Theories of Childhood

Other Redleaf Press books by Carol Garhart Mooney

Choose Your Words: How Teacher Talk Helps Children Learn, Second Edition

Theories of Childhood

An Introduction to Foundational Early Childhood Theorists

Revised and Expanded Third Edition

Carol Garhart Mooney
Erin Mooney Martin

Published by Redleaf Press
10 Yorkton Court
St. Paul, MN 55117
www.redleafpress.org

© 2000, 2013 by Carol Garhart Mooney and 2026 with Erin Mooney Martin

All rights reserved. Unless otherwise noted on a specific page, no portion of this publication may be reproduced or transmitted in any form or by any means, electronic or mechanical, including photocopying, recording, or capturing on any information storage and retrieval system, without permission in writing from the publisher, except by a reviewer, who may quote brief passages in a critical article or review to be printed in a magazine or newspaper, or electronically transmitted on radio, television, or the internet.

First edition published 2000. Second edition 2013. Third edition 2026.
Typeset by Douglas Schmitz
Author photo by Jeff Klapes
Printed in the United States of America
33 32 31 30 29 28 27 26   1 2 3 4 5 6 7 8

Library of Congress Cataloging-in-Publication Data
Names: Mooney, Carol Garhart author | Martin, Erin Mooney author
Title: Theories of childhood : an introduction to foundational early childhood theorists / Revised and Expanded Third Edition by Carol Garhart Mooney and Erin Mooney Martin.
Description: Revised and expanded third edition. | St. Paul, MN : Redleaf Press, [2026] | Revised and expanded edition of : Theories of childhood : an introduction to Dewey, Montessori, Erikson, Piaget, and Vygotsky, 2013. | Includes bibliographical references and index. | Summary: "Understand theories of childhood to make your days with children smoother, your job easier, and your program stronger. This best-selling resource provides clear, straightforward introductions to the foundational theories of John Dewey, Maria Montessori, Erik Erikson, Jean Piaget, Lev Vygotsky, and Janice E. Hale, as well as discussion of attachment theory. Each chapter highlights a theorist's work and includes insight on how the theory impacts teaching young children today"— Provided by publisher.
Identifiers: LCCN 2025045176 (print) | LCCN 2025045177 (ebook) | ISBN 9781605548500 paperback | ISBN 9781605548517 ebook
Subjects: LCSH: Early childhood education--Philosophy | Child development--Philosophy
Classification: LCC LB1139.23 .M64 2026 (print) | LCC LB1139.23 (ebook)
LC record available at https://lccn.loc.gov/2025045176
LC ebook record available at https://lccn.loc.gov/2025045177

Printed on acid-free paper

To our families: Marc, Gene, Cam, and Addie, this book would not be possible without your love and support.

Contents

Acknowledgments	ix
Introduction	xi
Chapter 1: Theories of Early Childhood Education	1
Chapter 2: John Dewey	9
Chapter 3: Maria Montessori	27
Chapter 4: Erik Erikson	43
Chapter 5: Jean Piaget	65
Chapter 6: John Bowlby	85
Chapter 7: Mary Ainsworth	95
Chapter 8: Lev Vygotsky	107
Chapter 9: Janice E. Hale	123
Chapter 10: Putting Theory to Practice	137
References	143
Index	149

Acknowledgments

REVISING *THEORIES OF CHILDHOOD* HAS BEEN BOTH a rewarding and challenging journey, and I am deeply grateful to all those who have walked alongside me through the process.

First and foremost, I want to thank my editor, Melissa York. Your thoughtful guidance, encouragement, and patience made all the difference. The dedication you brought to this project not only sharpened the manuscript but also helped bring clarity and coherence to my ideas. This book would not be what it is without your expertise and care.

I am also indebted to our interview participants, Colleen McKinnon and Dr. Lisa Ranfos. Colleen, through her leadership and perspective as a Black female leader, highlighted the importance of celebrating and honoring Black excellence within early educational settings. Dr. Ranfos, a lifelong learner and advocate for meaningful early childhood education in New Hampshire, illuminated the complexities of strong childcare institutions and the profound impact that high-quality early education can have on children and families. Thank you both for sharing your wisdom, time, and commitment to education and child development.

To my family—Gene, Addie, Cam, Marc, Dave, and Dee—your belief in me has kept me moving forward. Your love, encouragement, and patience gave me the strength I needed to finish this work.

Finally, I owe my deepest gratitude to my mom and coauthor, Carol Garhart Mooney. My mom has dedicated her life to advancing the instruction and best practices of early childhood education. I still remember, as a little girl, watching her run outside with sheer joy, holding her first published book, *Reflections on Parenting*, high in the air and shouting, "It's here! I did it!" That moment, and her decades

Acknowledgments

of research, writing, and teaching that followed, left an indelible mark on me. As an educator and researcher myself, it is the honor of my life to collaborate with her on this new edition of *Theories of Childhood*. Her influence on the field—and on the people fortunate enough to know and learn from her—is immeasurable. I am proud to carry her work forward and add to her legacy.

—**Erin Mooney Martin**

Introduction

Raising healthy children is a labor-intensive operation. Contrary to the news from the broader culture, most of what children need, money cannot buy. Children need time and space, attention, affection, guidance and conversation. They need sheltered places where they can be safe as they learn what they need to know to survive.

—Mary Pipher

My entire life has been dedicated to the profession of raising children in environments where they can thrive in developmentally appropriate ways. The first edition of *Theories of Childhood* was published in 2000, and as I have entered into my later years, I have collaborated with my daughter, Erin Mooney Martin, EdD, to continue the important work of researching child development and writing about it in a way that is comprehensible to those who are raising and working with young children. As the world continues to change, and as technology rapidly evolves, I thought it important to update my three books about theories of childhood development (*Theories of Childhood*, *Theories of Attachment*, and *Theories of Practice*). They are now combined into this single volume.

It isn't anyone's imagination that working with children is getting harder and harder. Despite our attempts at optimism, every experienced educator knows that the job was easier four decades ago. There are so many theories about why this is so that the topic could fill volumes. Jerome Kagan points out that in addition to the impact of both heredity (genes inherited from our birth parents) and the environment (people and places affecting our experiences after

Introduction

birth), psychologists are seeing more and more how society and culture at large affect growth and development (Kagan 1998).

What factors in US society affect the growth and development of our children? We live in one of the more violent countries of the developed world. Many people feel it is not safe to walk alone in their own neighborhoods at night. Parents and teachers are worried about their children and students. This concern is well founded. With continued acts of gun violence and school shootings, it has been reported the number one cause of death for young children is by guns (Johns Hopkins 2025).

Media influences and consumerism are often not in the best interest of our children. Myriad studies on the effects of media and film violence have reached the same conclusion: Television violence leads to real-world violence (New Hampshire Pediatric Association Newsletter, n.d.).

Family and community life have changed dramatically in the new millennium. Much of the public discussion of these changes has focused on the negative. People express fear that the family is endangered. Campaign slogans call for a return to family values. Yet, as Stephanie Coontz (2016) points out in *The Way We Never Were*, trying to solve today's challenges to family life through a return to "traditional" family forms is pointless. Americans, she writes, cherish a myth of stable, happy families that exist primarily in the minds of those who indulge in nostalgia. Families in every era have dealt with poverty, stress, death, illness, and emotional misunderstandings between family members. Child abuse, racism, and the inequities of class and gender are constants throughout our nation's history.

Nostalgia for "the good old days" is not an answer, but addressing the changes of our times is necessary. The technological changes to our daily lives in this century alone are astounding. Our challenge is to find adequate and creative ways to adapt to these changes. We spend less time with family and friends. The debates of the 1990s over quality time versus quantity time have disappeared. Today, for many, it is a stretch to find any time together! Many workplaces and community organizations have not kept pace with social changes. For example, numerous community organizations for children continue to hold events such as father-daughter dances or father-son campouts, ignoring the fact that fewer than half of all US families resemble the stereotypical family of two opposite-gender married parents with children living in a single household. Similarly, many schools have not creatively adapted their parent involvement components to match the lives of dual-career or single-parent families. Failure to adapt to these social changes stresses our children.

Another key change is the way children have been driven from the natural world by technological advances (social media), fear ("stranger danger," natural disasters), and even classroom messages meant to raise their concerns about the world's future (climate change). This phenomenon has been termed "nature-deficit disorder." In his book *Last Child in the Woods*, author Richard Louv (2008) writes, "Nature-deficit disorder describes the human costs of alienation from nature, among them: diminished use of the senses, attention difficulties, and higher rates of physical and emotional illnesses." Additionally, if children are not given opportunities to explore and embrace the natural world, who will take care of it in the future?

Twenty years ago, we didn't pay much attention to the ethnocentric nature (based on the attitude that one's own group is superior) of many of our considerations regarding children and families in the United States. Today we interpret all learning with a much broader lens as we consider culture, changing times, the importance of spending time in nature, and practices we didn't know existed even a decade ago.

By now, I'm sure you are asking, "What does all of this have to do with Piaget and Erikson?" Teachers in early childhood programs spend many hours discussing child and family struggles. Many of the teachers I talk with are discouraged. "The behavior problems are too much to handle," they tell me. Some of them blame parents.

Introduction

Some even make statements like "If parents don't want to care for their kids, then why do they have them?" This attitude usually comes from the frustration of having daily interactions with children in pain. When we can't make it better, we want someone to blame, and parents are an easy target. Many parents are stressed also. They know their long hours are taking a toll on family life. Like teachers, they often don't know what to do to make it better. This is where Erikson, Piaget, and the other theorists come in. When I ask teachers what they learned in college that might help them respond to children under stress, many of them just laugh. Some make comments such as "I could never keep all of those theorists straight" or "That textbook approach doesn't work once you're in a real classroom." Teachers will say, "Now, which one was he?" or "Wasn't Piaget the cognitive theory?" but rarely pause to reflect on how understanding child development theory might benefit their day-to-day classroom practices. The purpose of this book is to look for those benefits.

Joining Theory to Practice

Anthropologist and teacher Margaret Mead said in *Redbook* magazine in 1963, "If one cannot state a matter clearly enough so that an intelligent twelve-year-old can understand it, one should remain within the cloistered walls of the University and laboratory until one gets a better grasp of one's subject matter." The field of early childhood education (ECE) needs to listen to this wisdom.

"I need to drop this course," a student of mine told me recently. "I'm a full-time student, the single mother of a three-year-old, and I work at Pizza Hut on weekends. I don't have the time or patience to figure out what this means!" She thrust her child-development textbook onto my desk and pointed to a highlighted passage in the introductory chapter. It read, "The improvement of research tends to increase divergence in the treatment of evidence and to multiply mystification in the interpretation of specific findings. As research on a problem matures, the angles of vision multiply."

I shared with her my memorized interpretation: "It means studying children is really complicated. The more we learn, the more there is to understand about a single topic." The student looked annoyed. "Well, why can't they just say that?" she asked. Then in a sad and quiet voice, she added, "When I see words that I've never even heard of, I get discouraged and think I'm crazy to be going to college. The director at my center told me all that theory won't help me once I'm working with kids anyway."

As a teacher of child development, I am always alarmed when students share stories like this, which they do frequently. To leap from disregarding difficult texts that do a poor job of introducing the subject to disregarding the importance of theory in shaping practice seems a huge mistake. Knowing the theoretical foundations of ECE is critical to providing high-quality early care and education.

Not everyone agrees with me. Several years ago, a survey of child care directors was done in my state to guide the investment of training dollars. Many directors responded that they didn't care if teachers knew who Vygotsky or Erikson were but wanted teachers to know what to do when the children were hitting or biting each other. The point these directors missed is that teachers who know what to do when children are hitting or biting are teachers who understand child development. Many of the directors interviewed said such things as "When I hire those college students, they are full of theory but don't know what to do in the classroom. I'd rather hire someone with no college but a true enjoyment of young children." In addition, statements like these serve to affirm one perception of the early childhood profession, which is that early childhood teachers function primarily as babysitters and that little learning happens in early childhood classrooms. These statements detract from the important work teachers do every day with young children and ultimately limit our ability as educators to advocate for high-quality early childhood programs for all children. We need teachers who have both a true enjoyment of children and a true understanding of how they grow and learn. It seems that we have not been successful at presenting child development theory as a usable tool for working effectively with young children. Perhaps we need to take a different approach to introducing theory and its practice to the beginning student or teacher.

Most of us chuckle when we say, "Well, in theory . . ." because we all expect gaps between any theory and the way we are able to apply that theory in real life. But these gaps are part of our growing understanding of the complexity of growth and development. They are inevitable. This is not a good enough reason for practitioners to dismiss theory as irrelevant to their day-to-day work with children.

Jargon does not help students grasp the important ideas of Piaget or Erikson. Memorizing names and stages out of context does not build the bridge we need between child development and children. I know that too many classrooms offer this textbook approach to theory, because when I ask teachers what they remember about child development theories from their college classes, too many of them respond, "Very little!" Others will tell me they could never remember whether Erikson was the one who talked about feelings and Piaget about thought, or the other way around. I can picture these students chanting "Piaget, Swiss psychologist, cognitive development theory" as one might memorize state capitals and major rivers. Given this kind of introduction to theory, it is no wonder so many directors say, "Just send me someone who has good sense about kids!"

As directors struggle with staffing shortages and inadequately prepared teachers, it is important to them that teachers know basic development information, such as that babies always need to be held during feeding. Teachers may not need to know that Erik Erikson was born in Germany and brought us the psychosocial theory of development, but they will do their jobs better if they know holding babies while they are being fed helps the children develop trust in grown-ups. Theory needs to be real to the developing teacher. It needs to be tested in practice and adapted to the realities of individual children and classrooms. This ongoing process is what builds the bridge between theory and practice. When directors and teachers see how understanding child development theory makes their days with children smoother, their jobs easier, and their programs stronger, then they will value this knowledge.

About This Book

Theories of Childhood is a practitioner's manual as well as a college textbook. It is designed for the person working with young children who wants to better understand how children think and act and how to be more effective with them. It begins with a discussion of the interactive nature of theory and practice that is necessary to make both meaningful. It includes information about and reflection on the work of eight of the major contributors to the body of knowledge upon which our best practices in ECE are based. It is a basic introduction and is not intended to be academic or scholarly. I'm hoping to whet the appetite of those interested in the relationship of theory to practice and its impact on real children, teachers, and classrooms. For this reason, each chapter concludes with discussion questions and suggestions for further reading.

As Olivia Saracho (2023, 16) has emphasized, "Child development is not a unified field, with a single integrated set of theories, nor does one theory or set of theories predominate. Rather, there are many different competing theories in the field." Theories of development and attachment tell us why and how children act in specific ways. These theories are based on years of research. Theories of practice help practitioners know how to take that research and put it into place inside the home or classroom. Knowledge of theory and experience with how to use theory in practice give educators and folks who work with young children a bank of best practices. Like peanut butter and jelly, theory and practice go hand in hand. That

Introduction

is why I have taken my three books, *Theories of Childhood*, *Theories of Attachment*, and *Theories of Practice* and combined them into one larger textbook. Having all three in one edition allows educators to digest theory while also brainstorming ways to teach based on theoretical research.

When combining the three texts, I selected seminal works from theorists who continue to make an impact on ECE. Additionally, I have added a new theorist, Janice Hale. While researching early childhood development, I came across Anthony Broughton, a Black professor who found it challenging to learn about child development from only White developmental theorists. He noted "the realities of Black children/people are often interpreted and legitimized in academia when told by White scholars." His research revolves around honoring the ideas of Black intellectuals that explore many ways of "knowing and being a Black child through a Black lens" (Broughton 2020). His work introduced me to that of Janice Hale, who conducted extensive research on Black children and the cultural contexts in which Black children live and learn. Like Broughton, Hale looked at Piaget and the limited discussion on how development varies from culture to culture. She believed a theory needed to be developed to better understand the learning and growth of Black children. I have added the work of Hale to this book to underscore unique shared experiences and to elevate voices of Black leaders in ECE who have not been highlighted historically. However, this additional theory is not meant to uniformly or inflexibly describe all Black children and their culture, learning, and growth; they are not a monolith. Hale's work continues to inspire modern-day Black scholars such as Dr. Gloria Boutte and Dr. Kim Parker.

The stories shared here are from real classrooms where I have either worked or observed others at work. Each chapter provides the reader with background information on the theorist's life and work. Classroom stories illustrate the points of the original writings. This is not a comprehensive introduction to the field or even to the individual theorists. I hope that this brief introduction to early childhood's theoretical foundations will help you understand how child development affects how we work with children in early childhood programs and will encourage you to go on to the more in-depth readings.

Chapter 1: Theories of Early Childhood Education

Theories of ECE have played a significant role in practice for decades. For years I have been interested in the value of strong theoretical foundations in producing meaningful daily practices with children. Unfortunately, my years of observation tell me that too often teachers' practices become routine or mundane and lack the foundation that makes a curriculum rich and exciting for learners.

At a training series for experienced teachers on combining ECE theories with daily practices, my copresenters and I began to explore the needs and gaps in teachers' experience. The training evolved into focus groups on how teachers and programs blend theory and practice—or how they don't. We started the first sessions with two pretests. The first was a series of fill-in-the-blank questions (usually considered more difficult than multiple-choice or matching questions). Some of the questions were as follows:

1. America runs on _____.

2. I saw her on _____ *with the Stars*.

3. "Drink Coke; it's the _____ thing!"

And here are the answers:
1. Dunkin'
2. *Dancing*
3. real

Teachers enthusiastically tallied their scores. Then we asked them to stand if they had all correct answers. All participants had at least several answers correct.

Chapter 1

Then we gave a second pretest. It was a test matching ECE theorists to theories, and all correct pairs were in plain view. These were the choices:

Theorists	Stage
Vygotsky	cognitive development theory
Erikson	progressive education
Montessori	zone of proximal development
Piaget	psychosocial development
Dewey	independence and environment

Again, participants scored their pretests, and we asked those with five correct answers to stand. Not a single participant stood. We asked if anyone had missed just one or two answers, and a stunned silence fell over the group. We let the silence hang in the air. Every teacher in the room had gotten most or all of the matches wrong. These were mostly experienced teachers of young children, and all of them were acknowledging that they lacked understanding of foundational ECE theorists.

We spent the rest of the session talking together about what had happened and why. We discussed the fact that even faithful Starbucks buyers knew that America runs on Dunkin'. We questioned why the majority of respondents who correctly identified *Dancing with the Stars* said they had never watched the program. Why would teachers who were young when the Coke slogan was used remember it but not major ECE foundational theorists whom they'd learned about only four or five years ago? The group discussed the effects of culture and advertising on the things they hold in their minds without really thinking about them.

During the discussion of the second pretest, a participant suggested teachers do things automatically without linking them to what they learned in college. As an ECE instructor, I was uncomfortable with the suggestion that theorists might be less relevant than advertising slogans. The implication was that as students in college, the participants had memorized theorists but did not truly make connections between the work of these theorists and their own daily work with children. Participants seemed to believe they had not placed theory in a meaningful context. The discussions in our focus groups that day reflect what has become a much broader problem in the ECE field: Most of these teachers had several to many years of experience working with young children and their families, yet all of them admitted that often their desired approach and their actual implementation of ideas were too far apart. As we explored what it means to know theory and to have good practice, we began to focus on a major concern for our field—that as ECE teachers, many of us don't know or understand the theory behind our practices.

It seems that we—the teacher educators—have not successfully presented child development theory as a tool for working with young children more effectively. Perhaps we need to take a different approach to introducing theory and its practice to beginning students and teachers. ECE professionals who have mastered foundational theory understand how important significant adults' responses are to children in the early years (birth through age eight). They understand that children's early experiences and attachments first affect their brain growth patterns and later their mobility, curiosity, spirit of adventure, and inquiry. Often their knowledge of foundational theory comes from reading and reflecting on theorists such as Piaget, Erikson, and Montessori.

When I asked teachers about their ideas on theory and practice, here are some of the things they said:

- "Theories are what you learn about in college or workshops."
- "Practices are what you do."
- "Theories are what Piaget and Vygotsky wrote about."
- "Theories are outdated for today's kids and teachers."

Chapter 1

- "Theories are what the director makes you put in written plans."
- "Practices are what you do all the time that sometimes have nothing to do with theory."
- "Developmentally appropriate practice is a theory. Fingerpainting and movement are practices."
- "Constructivism is a theory."
- "We are still practicing our practices."
- "Theory is how you'd like it to be."
- "Practice is how it is."

Any experienced early educator has heard the following and many other comments that point to a general disrespect for the relationship between theory and positive practices:

- "Yeah, well, in theory."
- "The theory is great, but try doing it with eighteen five-year-olds!"
- "Yes, we are licensed for three- to six-year-olds, and yes, theoretically they are all independently toileting, but of course we have a changing table!"

Yet colleagues who work in ECE note it is clear to them that the more teachers know about theory and its implementation, the fewer struggles they have in their daily work with children. Easing one's own workload is not the first or most important reason for learning theory, though clearly that is a benefit.

The range of child development theories available today is vast and includes many aspects of human behavior. It can be a challenge for beginners to know where to start. A good place to begin is with the word *theory* itself. Like many words in our language, it means a variety of things to people. Often students respond to a theory as if it is an opinion no weightier than their own. We frequently hear people say, "I have a theory about that." What they typically mean is that they have a hypothesis—a first attempt at explaining something. Having a hypothesis about something is the initial spark of science and invention that leads to such amazing things as cures for polio, computers, cell phones, and social media. For a hypothesis to become a theory, it must be proven to be an accurate explanation through many tests. Saracho (2023) examines child development theory and notes that it "looks at the children's growth and behavior and interprets it. It suggests elements in the child's genetic makeup and the environmental conditions that influence development and behavior and how these elements are related."

Imagine a teacher who offers colleagues her hypothesis (she may call it a theory, but it is a hypothesis) that Ana, a student, is not getting enough sleep lately based on the following observations: She keeps rubbing her eyes, is crying more frequently than usual, and is not getting along with her favorite friends. The usual process would then be for colleagues to agree to observe Ana more closely and talk with her family members to see if she has been getting enough sleep. These actions would test the teacher's hypothesis that Ana's behavior and a lack of sleep are related. It would not, however, become a universal theory that children who cry frequently are tired, because the hypothesis is based on just one child's behavior. Ana's teacher develops the hypothesis because she notices something is wrong. This leads her to watch Ana more closely and then connect Ana's behavior to fatigue. Sharing this hypothesis with parents and other teachers in Ana's life could provide the information needed to confirm or disprove it. Even if confirmed, the hypothesis would not become a theory until it had been tested over time to collect data on a large population of children.

Chapter 1

Developing Theories from Research and Observation

If we ask where child development theories come from, we might consider the following pathways:

- data collected from direct observations of young children and then organized
- data carefully analyzed to predict patterns of behavior
- observations of children's conversations or drawings
- testing of hypotheses of previous studies (such as university-based, government-based, and cross-cultural studies)
- classical works and seminal studies

The foundational theories of early childhood growth and development are ideas that have held up over decades or even centuries. Theories can be brand-new too, but they must be based on research and created by careful observation and collection of data. It's important to acknowledge the difference between the personal hypotheses we develop in our own classrooms drawn from a specific group of children and the theories considered to be universal in the ECE field. To do our best for the children and families in our care, we need to bring to our daily work both the documented research of the ECE field as well as our own hypotheses gleaned from observations and interactions.

The foundational theories in ECE are many. Some of the theories based on older studies have been found inadequate when applied to today's children and families. Some resonate as strongly today as when they were proposed. Theorists look at human behavior through different lenses, so no one theory is universally accepted as the best explanation of how and why children grow and learn as they do. Many educators take an eclectic approach to child development theory, basing their ideas on a broad and diverse range of sources. When teachers care about providing a high-quality experience for children, understanding and growing with the theories of practice are necessary parts of the job.

Working professionally with other people's children means acknowledging and respecting these important guidelines and methods so we can do our best for the next generation. Loving children and enjoying their company are as essential as knowing theories of child growth and development. Both are necessary for continuous improvement in our work as early childhood educators. The following chapters explain specific foundational theories, show how these theories can be put into practice, and describe their impact on real children, educators, and classrooms.

Chapter 2: John Dewey

The fundamental issue is not of new versus old education nor of progressive against traditional education but a question of what anything whatever must be to be worthy of the name education.

—John Dewey, *Experience and Education*

Biography

BORN IN 1859 IN Burlington, Vermont, John Dewey was a US educator who has significantly influenced our thinking about education in this country. Dewey's family had farmed in Vermont for three generations. He attended the University of Vermont, where he studied philosophy. In 1884 he received a PhD at Johns Hopkins University, which led to a teaching position at the University of Michigan. While serving as a professor of philosophy there, he became friends with one of his students, Alice Chipman. They were married in 1886, and it was largely Chipman's influence that brought Dewey to the study of education. She was interested in social problems and their relationship to education. Her interest was contagious, and soon she and Dewey were working together to determine the best ways to support the education of children in the United States.

In 1894 they moved to the University of Chicago, where Dewey took a position teaching philosophy. He found the position desirable because it was intended that he blend the teaching of philosophy with both psychology and educational theory. Within two years, he had established a famous laboratory school that attracted attention

Chapter 2

around the world. Dewey's laboratory school established the University of Chicago as the center of thought on progressive education, the movement toward more democratic and child-centered education. Progressive education was a reaction to the traditional rigid, formal style of education common during the nineteenth century. Progressive education was considered genius by many and criticized as too radical by others. Dewey's involvement with the lab school was relatively short-lived but created, in a few years, a wealth of educational research and theory that continues to drive many of our best practices today.

In 1904, arguing with administrators over education budgets, Dewey resigned his position at the University of Chicago. He took a post at Columbia University in New York City, where he continued to teach and write for another four decades. Dewey contributed volumes of work to our knowledge base in educational psychology and theory. Much of his work is as relevant today to the struggles of US educators as it was many decades ago. His writings cover a broad range of educational topics. Dewey continued writing and revising manuscripts until his death in 1952 at the age of ninety-three.

In 1899 John Dewey gave a talk to the parents his students. The parents were worried about the changing times. It was a time of great industrial growth in the United States, and these parents were old enough to remember a more agricultural era. They remembered when children were educated at home by watching their parents do meaningful work. They thought the new generation lacked character and values. Dewey agreed with parents that the home was no longer educating children in the way it had in the past, but he gave them good counsel: "We cannot overlook the factors of discipline and of character building involved . . . but it is useless to bemoan the departure of the good old days of children's modesty, reverence, and implicit obedience, if we expect merely by bemoaning the exhortation to bring them back" (Dewey 1899, 19–20).

Dewey was trying to get his parent group to understand that while change brings new problems, it also brings opportunities. He urged parents to think of new ways they could all find to help children learn to be socially responsible people without trying to cling to times gone by.

At the end of the next century, teachers were struggling with the very same issues. In her 1997 publication *Dewey's Laboratory School: Lessons for Today*, Laurel Tanner points out that a century ago Dewey asked the questions we still seek answers to in the twenty-first century: How do we best introduce children to subject matter? Should we have multiage classrooms? How can we best plan curriculum? How can supervisors support classroom teachers? How should thinking skills be taught? Significant answers to these and similar questions about teaching can be found in Dewey's many volumes. Dewey's work is echoed in the writings of many modern educational theorists. As we speak today of dispositions for learning, purposeful curricula, shaping experiences through well-planned environments, and many other theoretical and practical conditions of teaching, we are discussing the issues that interested Dewey and that he wrote and talked about.

Dewey is most closely associated with the US progressive education movement, playing a central role in its development. In Europe Maria Montessori and Jean Piaget were spreading the same message. These early theorists all agreed that children learn from doing and that education should involve real-life materials and experiences and should encourage experimentation and independent thinking. These ideas, now quite common, were considered revolutionary in Dewey's day.

Dewey's Theories

John Dewey wrote so many volumes on the philosophy and practice of education that an introductory text cannot begin to cover his contribution to our field. As a progressive educator, he shared with Vygotsky, Montessori, and Piaget the central ideas of that movement: Education should be child-centered; education must be both active and interactive; and education must involve the social world of the child and the community. In 1897 Dewey published his philosophy of education in a document called *My Pedagogic Creed* (Dewey 1897). Here's what he said about education:

> **"True education comes through the stimulation of the child's powers by the demands of the social situations in which he finds himself"** (3). Dewey believed that children learn best when they interact with other people, working both alone and cooperatively with peers and adults.
>
> **"The child's own instincts and powers furnish the material and give the starting-point for all education"** (4). According to Dewey, children's interests form the basis for curriculum planning. He believed that the interests and background of each child and group must be considered when teachers plan learning experiences.
>
> **"I believe that education, therefore, is a process of living and not preparation for future living"** (7). Dewey believed that education is part of life. He believed that as long as people are alive, they are learning, and that education should address what the person needs to know at the time, not prepare them for the future. Dewey thought that curriculum should grow out of real home, work, and other life situations.
>
> **"The school life should grow gradually out of the home life. . . . It is the business of the school to deepen and extend [the child's] sense of values bound up in his home life"** (7–8). Dewey thought teachers must be sensitive to the values and needs of families. What happens at school should reflect and deepen the values and cultures of families and communities.
>
> **"I believe, finally, that the teacher is engaged, not simply in the training of individuals, but in the**

formation of a proper social life" (18). Dewey believed that teachers do not teach just subject matter but also how to live in society. In addition, he thought that teachers do not just teach individual children but also shape the society.

It is the last piece of Dewey's pedagogic creed that is the springboard for some of his most provocative ideas. He believed that teachers need to have confidence in their skills and abilities. He believed teachers need to trust their knowledge and experience and, using both, provide appropriate activities to nurture inquiry and dispositions for learning in the children they work with.

The Teacher's Role

In *Experience and Education*, Dewey (1938) said that teachers should have more confidence when planning children's learning experiences. He said teachers were too afraid that instruction would infringe upon the freedom and creativity of their students. Dewey thought that children need assistance from teachers in making sense of their world.

What should this assistance look like? Dewey thought it was important for teachers to observe children and to determine from these observations what kinds of experiences the children are interested in and ready for. He thought that the educator has a serious responsibility to invest in planning and organizing for children's learning activities. In other words, he believed that it is the teacher's job to determine the curriculum based on knowledge of the children and their abilities. He felt that suggestions and guidance coming from thoughtful teachers, who, after all, have more life experience and more general knowledge than children, could not possibly be less useful to children than the ideas they arrive at by accident.

When progressive education was criticized for allowing children too much freedom without appropriate guidance, Dewey agreed.

Chapter 2

"It is a ground for legitimate criticism . . . when the ongoing movement of progressive education fails to recognize that the problem of selection and organization of subject matter for study and learning is fundamental," he responded (Dewey 1938, 78). Dewey was saying that children need teachers to decide what is safe and what is developmentally and individually appropriate for them.

Dewey was concerned that many teachers of his time were claiming to be part of progressive education merely because they departed from more traditional approaches. He recognized the danger in changing direction without clearly understanding the new direction one wanted to follow. He also thought this was a common pattern among educators. He believed some teachers were drawn to progressive education because they thought it would be easier. He knew that they used the new ideas as justification for improvising or allowing children to choose their experiences, uninhibited by teacher planning or direction.

Dewey believed that the path to high-quality education is to know the children well, to build their experiences on past learning, to be organized, and to plan carefully. He also believed that observing, documenting, and keeping records of classroom events are much more important when using this new method than when traditional methods are used. Today these beliefs and many others articulated by Dewey are foundational pieces of developmentally appropriate practice (DAP) and emergent and constructivist early childhood curriculum models.

Dewey believed that to provide educational experiences for children, teachers must

- have a strong base of general knowledge as well as knowledge of specific children;
- be willing to use their greater knowledge and experience to make sense of the world for children; and
- invest in observation, planning, organization, and documentation.

How can Dewey's theory about the teacher's role in education guide you in your early childhood program?

- Observe children closely and plan curriculum from their interests and experience.

- Don't be afraid to use your knowledge of the children and the world to make sense of the world for children.

Plan Purposeful Curriculum

Once when I was visiting a group of four-year-olds, I noticed a child who spent most of her free time crawling about the room. She would say, "Meow," to anyone she passed. She did not play with other children. She did not seek interaction from her teacher. She simply roamed around meowing. I asked the teacher about this child.

"She likes to think she's a cat," the teacher said.

"Why is that?" I asked.

"I'm not sure," the teacher said.

"Does she have a cat at home?" I asked.

"I'm not sure," the teacher said again.

"Do you ever wonder what makes her do it?" I pushed.

"She really enjoys it . . . and that's enough for me," the teacher said, smiling confidently, and added, "Learning should be fun!"

This is not what Dewey meant by teacher confidence! He said that confidence should spring from the base of knowledge that the teacher applies to classroom situations. That knowledge includes knowing the child (Does she have a cat?); individualizing curricula (Does she need to work through the death of a pet?); understanding the social nature of learning (How can the teacher or peers help or join her?); and preparation for life (What is the point of this behavior? How and what is she learning from it that she can use as she goes through life?).

Dewey certainly believed that when children were engaged, learning was fun and exciting in and of itself. However, in this example, the teacher was content to accept "fun" as a justification for aimless activity without trying to understand the meaning of the experience for the child. The teacher did not build on the child's preoccupation with being a cat to extend her knowledge of the world, to advance her skills, or to support her development. She did not connect the child's interest to her own broad knowledge of the world or to learning that had gone before. Using Dewey's criteria and terminology, this would be a "mis-educative" experience (Dewey 1938, 25).

This is similar to the misconception among some early childhood educators today that a hands-on curriculum is enough. In *The Young Child as Scientist: A Constructivist Approach to Early Childhood Science Education,* authors Christine Chaillé and Lory Britain (2003, 17) write, "The constructivist [teacher] sees the essential activity as what goes on in the child's head, not in his or her hands. With young children, physical activity and manipulation is often a necessary part of mental activity, but not always. . . . Children need to be active, yes, and they need opportunities to manipulate and experiment with real objects. But this in itself is not the definition of a good activity."

Here's a different example: In a classroom where five-year-olds were at work, I observed some children playing with glue. At first glance, this activity seemed aimless as well as wasteful. The children had taken empty thread spools from the art area. Placing a finger under the bottom hole, they filled the spool with glue. Quickly turning it sideways, the children blew the glue out of the hole. "Wow, you did it, just like yesterday!" one child shouted exuberantly as the glue spread across the art table.

Fascinated, I was wondering what kind of curriculum the school followed when the teacher quickly intervened. "You must be showing our visitor what you did with eggs yesterday," she said. She explained that the children had been looking at decorated eggs from around the world. The teacher had shown them how the artists prepare the eggshells by blowing out the raw egg inside. Now the children's behavior made sense to me. Then the teacher said, "You really understood that process with the eggs. You have done the same thing with the spools and glue. We can't use up all of our glue, though, so I want you to put that away now. Then we can go check on our eggs from yesterday and see if they are ready to decorate."

This teacher knew her students well. She knew exactly what they were doing and why. She affirmed the connection between the eggs and the glue and then redirected the children to the original project. She wasn't afraid to say, "I see what you are doing. It makes sense, but let's not do it with glue. Let's get back to our eggs." Her guidance ensured that the experimenting was turned from mere *experience* to *learning experience*. This is the teacher confidence Dewey speaks of. It is based on knowledge both of specific children and of the learning process.

Make Sense of the World for Children

Dewey also said that beyond their knowledge of children, teachers must be willing to tap their general knowledge of the world to help children make sense of their surroundings and experiences. This is a challenge for many early childhood teachers, who have often been discouraged from sharing their knowledge with children.

For example, I was at a statewide gathering of Head Start teachers who were working toward their Child Development Associate Credential. As part of the seminar, teachers were reflecting on the project work they were doing with children. One teacher, Kathy, talked about her class's investigation of winter birds. The children had observed and commented on the V formation of birds flying above the play area. Their teachers explained that the birds were going south for the winter. The children knew that not all birds left New England because birds visited their bird feeder daily, and this launched the class into a project studying the birds that remained in the area during the winter.

Kathy showed the group some cardinals that the children had made. They were so realistic that at first no one guessed they were made from paper plates, painted and feathered. Several teachers also commented that they looked as if they had been made by older children.

Some of the teachers were disturbed by Kathy's presentation. "Did you use a model?" one asked.

"No," Kathy responded. "We had the children carefully observe the cardinals in the yard. We brought in lots of books with pictures and photographs, and when we set up the activity, we set out only materials and paint appropriate to making cardinals."

The discussion got more heated. "You actually did this with five-year-olds? I can't believe you would only set out red and brown paint! What if someone wanted theirs to be purple or green? Isn't this whole thing infringing on the children's creativity?" There was an explosion of questions and comments.

Kathy was tentative. Her head teacher had warned her that some of her peers might not understand or approve of the work they were doing with the class. Quietly she shared their approach. "We didn't put green paint out because there aren't green cardinals. There has been a lot of painting and drawing in other areas of the classroom, but we think of this project as scientific investigation, not creative arts. We are studying birds, what they look like, what they eat, where they live. We want the children to know more about some of the birds that live in their backyards, and we thought it was important to share accurate information. Restricting the colors they painted with for this project has actually made their study more interesting. Last week I overheard a child tell her classmate, as they stared out the window, 'That must be a blue jay. It can't be a cardinal because they are all red!'"

This was followed by another burst of comments: "Isn't it inappropriate to tell children what color they should use on a project? If children are painting, shouldn't they use whatever color they want? Well, but bird-watching is different from easel painting. Do we really want children pointing to a pigeon and saying, 'There's a cardinal'? If a child brought you a picture of an octopus and it only had six tentacles, would you correct her? Would you say, 'That's wrong; go back and add two more tentacles'?"

Kathy responded slowly and thoughtfully. "We wouldn't say, 'It's wrong, go back and fix it!' but we might say some other thought-provoking things. We would have many books about sea life with drawings and photographs. We might say something like, 'Let's look at your drawing of the octopus and the pictures in *National Geographic*.' We might call attention to the fact that these creatures sure have more legs than we do! Many children would then begin counting and would realize that a real octopus has eight tentacles. This is the kind of discovery that learning is all about!"

Not all the other teachers were convinced. A long discussion ensued: "Process is what is important to young children. Each child's work should look the way she wants it to. This whole approach seems manipulative. We *never* tell children how to draw. This doesn't seem very developmentally appropriate!"

Kathy explained to the group that the teachers at her center had visited the Hundred Languages of Children traveling exhibition. They had been amazed at some of the work done by preschoolers in Reggio Emilia, Italy. After attending project seminars, the staff had reflected on their current work with the children. Their new learning convinced them that they had been underestimating what the children were capable of. "We decided that, as teachers, our responsibility includes making sense of the world to children even if it means having them take another look at the color of birds or their two-legged horses!" she concluded.

Kathy's story is a good example of what Dewey meant by teachers using their greater knowledge to help the children make sense of their world. Children in her classroom have ample opportunity for unfettered creative expression, but in the study she described, children were using art as a tool for scientific investigation. By helping the children look closely at the birds they were studying and giving them the tools to make accurate representations of them, these teachers built on the children's knowledge. They helped the children learn more about the birds. They also gave the children skills they could use for future investigations. This, according to Dewey, is how teachers should use their knowledge of the world to expand children's knowledge.

Education Versus Miseducation

Dewey avoided the either-or discussions so common to educational philosophy. He believed that the real issue is not a matter of new versus old approaches to education, but rather what conditions make any experience worthy of being called educational. Dewey insisted that education and experience are related but not equal, and that some experiences are not educational at all. He called these miseducative experiences. Dewey believed that an activity is not a learning activity if it lacks purpose and organization. He criticized the more traditional formal teaching environments of the nineteenth and early twentieth centuries, in which children learned information by rote and spent days reciting facts out of context. He also criticized situations in which teachers set up the learning environment and then turn children loose to explore without offering any guidance or suggestions, and those in which teachers set up experiences randomly without providing any unifying theme, continuity, or purpose. Dewey thought that rather than saying, "The children will enjoy this," teachers need to ask the following questions when they plan activities for children:

- How does this expand on what these children already know?
- How will this activity help this child grow?
- What skills are being developed?
- How will this activity help these children know more about their world?

- How does this activity prepare these children to live more fully?

From Dewey's perspective, an experience can only be called educational if it meets these criteria:

- It is based on the children's interests and grows out of their existing knowledge and experience.
- It supports the children's development.
- It helps the children develop new skills.
- It adds to the children's understanding of their world.
- It prepares the children to live more fully.

How can you be guided by Dewey's criteria for educational experiences?

- Do not accept "It's fun" as a sole justification for curriculum, but ask how an activity will support children's development and learning. It is not enough for an activity to be hands-on; it must be minds-on as well.
- Invest in organization and documentation.

"It's Fun" Is Not Enough

Dewey believed that when people are engaged in learning something that interests them and is related to their experience, the process of learning is enjoyable. However, he also said that enjoyment alone is not enough to make an experience educational. Teachers can use Dewey's criteria to make sure the experiences they plan for children are not just "fun" but also build children's learning.

For example, I once visited a classroom where children were having a make-your-own-sundae celebration. There was much excitement in the room. Children told me they could choose frozen yogurt or ice cream, sprinkles or M&Ms, chocolate syrup or strawberries. The teacher did a survey at the end of the day, asking children which flavor was their favorite. She had carefully prepared a poster. It said, "Our Favorite Ice Cream!" She had cut out ice-cream cones in brown, white, and pink. The children chose cones and put their names on them. When the teacher called their names, they placed their cones next to the words *chocolate*, *vanilla*, or *strawberry*. As Zachary taped his brown cone to the chart, he smiled and said, "My favorite is Cherry Garcia."

Later I asked the teacher how she thought the activity had gone. Like so many teachers I speak with, she said, "The children really seemed to enjoy it." When I asked why she had planned this particular activity, she smiled and said, "I knew they would love it!"

Dewey would say this teacher had not done enough planning for this activity. It's unclear whether the children had expressed an interest in ice cream, or how the activity built on any prior information they had. What did they already know about ice cream? What were they curious about? It's also hard to see how the activity supported children's development or helped them learn new skills. The documentation of the activity was limited to the chart, which was inaccurate—the only choices were chocolate, vanilla, and strawberry, which didn't reflect Zachary's favorite, Cherry Garcia, and his choice of a brown cone required no association of colors with flavors. In addition, by concluding the activity with a chart of favorite flavors, the teacher had not left the children wondering or searching for more.

Invest in Organization and Documentation

A different teacher turned the same subject, ice cream, into a lesson Dewey would probably have identified as a learning experience. This kindergarten teacher had invited a parent to come in and share an old family recipe for peach ice cream. In preparing the children for this visit, she discovered that none of the children had ever tasted peach ice cream before. The teacher asked the children why they thought no one had ever tasted it, and she documented their answers. Here are some of them:

- "It's not at the store."
- "It's a fruit, not an ice cream."
- "I'm allergic!"
- "Chocolate is best."

The teacher asked the children more questions: "Do you eat much ice cream? What is your favorite flavor? Have you ever made ice cream?" Then she asked the children to talk to their families about ice cream. The next day, the list of answers was longer: Tom's dad liked rocky road; Heather had gone to the Ben & Jerry's factory to watch them make ice cream; Nina's grandmother liked orange sherbet, which is sort of like ice cream but not exactly!

When the parent came in to help the children make peach ice cream, she used an old-fashioned ice-cream maker that had been her grandmother's. Children took turns mixing the ingredients and turning the crank. The teacher asked the children if they thought this was how the ice cream they got at the store was made, and she documented their responses. Here are some of the things they said:

- "No—it's too slow."
- "It's not big enough to make all those ice creams."
- "They have to use gigantic bowls."
- "They don't turn the handle like this; they use a huge mixer like when my mom makes cake."

The teacher observed from these responses that the children did not know how ice cream could be made in large quantities. She saw that they were unable to make connections between the ice cream they were making at school and the idea of an ice-cream factory.

Chapter 2

She asked the children how they might find out how huge quantities of ice cream are made, and she wrote down what they said. Among their answers were these:

- "Watch somebody do it."
- "Call the supermarket and ask them!"
- "Ask the cook."
- "Look on the internet."
- "Go to Ben & Jerry's."

The teacher tried to follow up on the children's suggestions. They visited an ice-cream and yogurt factory. They talked to other people and each other about ice cream. The body of information kept growing. Grandparents shared stories of eating ice cream all day after having their tonsils removed as children. The children wrote stories, drew pictures, collected recipes, took field trips, and took photographs to document all this learning.

This class also had a make-your-own-sundae party. Families were invited. The children served the peach ice cream. The room was decorated with their charts, graphs, stories, and pictures. This party was a celebration of weeks of learning about something familiar to everyone. Meanwhile, the children were already talking about their next project for study: refrigeration! During the ice-cream study, Emily's grandfather had told her about cutting ice from nearby New Hampshire lakes in winter to store and use for iceboxes in summer. Many of the children had never heard of refrigeration without electricity. They all swam in the lake where Emily's grandfather had cut ice in the "old days." They were fascinated by this story and curious about how food was kept fresh before electrical refrigeration was available. Their learning was spiraling in new directions.

This story is an example of what Dewey would call an educational experience. The teacher observed and asked questions to determine the children's prior knowledge. She set up experiences for them to discover things they didn't already know. She used her knowledge of child development to plan curriculum that was age appropriate, and she documented the children's learning to support her understanding of their thinking. The project was successful because it led into the next area of study. It left the children curious, wanting more, and confident in their ability to dive in and satisfy their curiosity.

In his book *My Pedagogic Creed*, Dewey references the need for teachers to teach children how to live in society. He believed that by shaping individual children, teachers shape society as well. Dewey supported parents during a time when US culture was transitioning from agricultural to industrial. As we ponder his important theory about shaping society as we teach young children, we can apply it to the fact that we are transitioning again as a culture. Teaching young children to care for the planet is not only interesting and relevant to the twenty-first century but essential to our survival. Why not extend those Earth Day celebrations to include planting seeds to improve air quality or discuss why electric vehicles are becoming more popular on today's roads?

To learn from and utilize Dewey's theories of education, we must be willing to change with the times. When Dewey appealed to parents and teachers of his day to adapt to societal changes rather than fighting them, he was offering sound advice. It does not help to mourn the past or dread new trends that might make us uncomfortable.

Discussion Questions

1. Progressive education has been called many things. What are some of the misconceptions about it? Give a brief explanation that summarizes Dewey's ideas about progressive education.

2. Today one common curriculum model is emergent curriculum, or planning curriculum around what emerges from the

children's interests and experiences. Is this consistent or inconsistent with Dewey's idea about education? Why?

3. Many families want an overtly structured environment for their children and feel anxious if they think that the children play too much. Using Dewey's ideas, prepare a response for families that illustrates the learning structure behind your program.

Suggestions for Further Reading

Dalton, Thomas C. 2002. *Becoming John Dewey: Dilemmas of a Philosopher and Naturalist.* Indiana University Press.

Dewey, John, and Evelyn Dewey. 1915. *Schools of To-morrow.* E. P. Dutton.

Johnston, James Scott. 2006. *Inquiry and Education: John Dewey and the Quest for Democracy.* State University of New York Press.

Moore, Philip B. 2025. *John Dewey: Prophet of an Educated Democracy.* Routledge.

Chapter 3: Maria Montessori

What is the greatest height of a Montessori teacher's success?
To be able to say: "Now the children work as if I did not exist."

—Maria Montessori, *The Absorbent Mind*

Biography

MARIA MONTESSORI WAS BORN in Chiaravalle, Italy, in 1870. She was the only daughter of wealthy, well-educated parents. Her mother always encouraged her to think and study and pursue a professional career. Her father, a conservative man, did not like having his daughter break with the traditional expectations for women of her era. He wanted Montessori to become a teacher, the only professional avenue considered appropriate for women at the time. However, he continued to support her when she became a student of science instead. She went on to medical school, where she constantly struggled with the resentment of male medical students and her father's disapproval. As time passed, Montessori's scholarship earned the respect of her classmates. She specialized in pediatrics during her last two years, and in 1896 she became the first woman in Italy to graduate from medical school.

Montessori's first job was to visit asylums and select patients for treatment. This was where her interest in young children and their needs developed. She noticed that children who had been diagnosed as "unteachable" responded to her methods. Because she had trained as a scientist, she used observation to determine the needs of the children. She was a brilliant woman and an astute observer. Soon

Chapter 3

she determined that the problems existed not in the children, but in the adults, in their approaches and in the environments they provided. By this time, Montessori was developing a reputation for her gifts with children and education. She was referred to as "Teacher." Many forgot that her training was in medicine.

Montessori's first opportunity to work with typically developing children came in 1907 when she opened her first Casa dei Bambini (Children's House) in the slums of Rome. The building was offered to Montessori as an attempt to keep the children of working parents out of the streets. Shop owners thought it would reduce vandalism. The children not only came in from the streets; they also became avid learners who loved to work and study. Montessori created a school environment to make up for the impoverished conditions of many of the children's homes. She determined that to be comfortable, young children need furnishings and tools that fit their small bodies and hands. Because such things were not available at the time, Montessori made many of her own materials. She learned from her students. She wrote about her observations and theories and developed an international reputation for her work. By 1913 there were almost one hundred schools in the United States following Montessori's methods. In 1922 she was appointed a government inspector of schools in Italy. Her opposition to Mussolini's fascism forced her to leave the country in 1934.

Maria Montessori was nominated for the Nobel Peace Prize three times. When she died in the Netherlands in 1952, she left educators of every nation a legacy of ideas and a collection of writings that still affect current practice in programs for young children.

Montessori's Theories

Many of Montessori's ideas are so basic to the ways we think about early childhood today that we take them for granted. Yet in 1907, when Dr. Montessori opened her first school, child-size furnishings and tools and the idea of children working independently were considered radical. Her research into young children and what they need in order to learn has affected the fundamental ways early educators think about children. Her work provided a foundation for the work of later theorists, such as Piaget and Vygotsky. Many of the ideas held by people who work in ECE today can be traced to Montessori.

In the United States, some early childhood programs call themselves Montessori programs. Some of them hold firmly to Montessori's principles, and some of them would never meet her standards. It is important to understand that Montessori's theories about children have influenced the structures of many early childhood programs today, not just those that call themselves Montessori programs. Montessori's theories are important to early childhood teachers no matter what programs they work in.

Child-Centered Environments

Montessori acknowledged that the emphasis she placed on preparation of the environment was probably the main characteristic by which people identified her method. She believed that the environment includes not only the space the children use and the furnishings and materials within that space but also the adults and the children who share their days with each other. Montessori believed that children learn language and other significant life skills without conscious effort from the environments where they spend their time. For that reason, she thought that environments for children need to be beautiful and orderly so that children can learn order from them. She believed children learn best through sensory experiences. She thought that the teacher has a responsibility to provide wonderful sights, textures, sounds, and smells for children. She also believed that sensory experiences for children should include having tools and utensils that fit their small hands and tables and chairs that match their small bodies. Beautiful, orderly, child-size environments and sensory play are part of Montessori's legacy.

Chapter 3

Most US early childhood programs have child-size furnishings, equipment, and utensils. What else can teachers learn from Montessori's understanding of good environments for children? Montessori thought that early childhood teachers should do the following:

- Provide real tools that work, such as sharp knives, good scissors, and woodworking and cleaning tools.

- Keep materials and equipment accessible to the children, organized so children can find and put away what they need.

- Create beauty and order in the classroom.

Provide Real Tools That Work
Montessori suggested that the size of furnishings and materials for children was important. When she opened her schools in Italy, child-size tools and furnishings were not available. This was why she became so involved in making her own materials. Montessori took this part of environment planning so seriously that even the staircase in her school was custom designed to fit her students' small feet. When we see classrooms outfitted with child-size hammers, saws, and workbenches, we are looking at Montessori's influence. Child-size pitchers and small mixing bowls and pots also demonstrate her ideas.

The fact that these child-size tools really work is also part of Montessori's educational philosophy. She believed children needed real tools if they were to do the real work that interested them so. In US preschools, children are often expected to cut paper with dull scissors and cut vegetables with butter knives so they won't get hurt. Unfortunately, these dull tools make these simple tasks more difficult, and in some cases more dangerous, than if children use sharp tools properly. Montessori believed that children could learn to use tools safely and that giving them tools that didn't really work undermined their competence.

Keep Materials and Equipment Accessible to the Children

In addition to having real tools, Montessori stressed the need for children to be able to reach materials when they wanted them so children could become responsible for their own learning. Arranging classrooms with low, open shelves means children can see what is available and get what they want without assistance from the teacher. They do not have to interrupt their work to get the attention of the busy teacher or ask permission to use the materials they need.

Often in US preschools, supplies are kept out of the children's reach. For example, teachers plan an art activity and get the paint out instead of having paint available all the time for children to use. Teachers following Montessori's lead have ample supplies available for children to use. With help from the children, they keep these supplies well organized so that choices and opportunities continually invite the children to be creative.

Often when teachers hesitate to arrange materials in an accessible way, they say it is because the children would make too much mess. Montessori (1949, 395) made it clear that it is a serious teaching responsibility to become "the guardian and custodian of the environment." She believed that the teacher should prepare a clean, organized, and orderly environment for the children. If every material has a place that is clearly marked in a child-friendly way with photographs or drawings as well as the printed name of the material that belongs there, children have the power to get what they need and to put it away when they are done.

Create Beauty and Order

Montessori used the word *cheerful* to describe well-planned spaces for children. She believed caring for the environment and keeping it bright and orderly should be viewed as a teaching skill. In the United States, teachers sometimes view cleaning and organizing as additional work that's not in their job description. According to Montessori, knowing how to arrange an interesting, beautiful environment for children is as much a part of teaching as knowing how to select fine children's books for the library. Montessori (1949, 182) said, "Our apparatus for educating the senses offers the child a key to guide his exploration of the world."

Ask yourself what you are providing in the environment to educate the senses. What sights and sounds do children hear when they enter the room? What is available to touch or taste? What music do you play? Do you bring in lilacs when they are in bloom? Do you open the windows and let the fresh air in? Does soft lamplight offer a break from the constant glare and hum of fluorescent lights? Are your displays of children's art carefully hung? Do you have a color scheme in your room, or does the purple shelf Josh's family donated sit next to the blue shelves the toddler room gave you because they didn't want them anymore? Were fundraising monies used to buy a lovely and comfortable new sofa, or are you using the one donated because the springs stick through the dirty upholstery and no adult would sit on it?

Adults sometimes act as if children have no interest in the beauty of their surroundings. They accept the stereotype that children like to mess up but not clean up. Observations of young children do not bear this out. Montessori believed that beauty and order are critical to prepared environments for children. That message is echoed today in the work of educators inspired by the teachers of Reggio Emilia, Italy.

For example, if children's paintings are matted on colored paper that brings out their colors, and if they are hung in a special display area, the children will learn to appreciate color and design. Another example is bringing in fresh flowers to grace the lunch table or the top of the bookcase. Walking in a field to pick flowers to make the classroom lovely is a fine way to spend a morning.

One Head Start teacher I know hangs a print of a famous still life painting in her studio area each week. She sets up similar still life items nearby. Some children try to draw them. Some children talk about the items. Others don't seem to notice the display, yet its presence communicates respect for beauty as part of the children's day.

Competence and Responsibility

Montessori believed that children want and need to care for themselves and their surroundings. She believed that adults spend too much time "serving" children. She cautioned teachers to remember that children who are not allowed to do something for themselves do not learn how to do it. Montessori understood that it is sometimes much easier to do something for a child than it is to take the time and energy to teach them to do it. But she also believed that for children to grow and develop skills, the adults in their lives need to make opportunities for children to do things for themselves. Fostering independence is part of Montessori's legacy.

Montessori believed that children learn best by doing and through repetition; children do things over and over to make an experience their own as well as to develop skills. Montessori urged teachers not to interfere with the child's patterns and pace of learning. She thought it was the teacher's job to prepare the environment, provide appropriate materials, and then step back and allow children the time and space to experiment. Open-ended scheduling, with large blocks of time for free work and play, is part of Montessori's legacy.

How can you apply Montessori's thinking about competence and responsibility in your programs?

- Give children responsibility for keeping the community space clean and orderly.

- Provide large blocks of time for free work and play, and allow children to structure their own time.

Allow Children to Take Responsibility

Montessori was convinced that the more we manage for children, the harder our jobs will be. Children have a passionate interest in real work. They love to watch the cook, the custodian, and the garbage collector at work. They always want to help. Montessori believed that children should be allowed and encouraged to do everything they are capable of. She believed it is the teacher's responsibility to increase each child's competence whenever possible.

Child care teachers often feel frustration that they are unable to do as much cleaning and organizing in their rooms as they want to. They feel frustrated and overwhelmed when the Legos, Unifix cubes, and pattern blocks get all mixed up and out of place. Many teachers plan sorting activities, never thinking to give the children the task of sorting materials into their proper place in the classroom. Teachers know that water play is calming for children, yet they worry about making time to clean because they are too busy planning activities for the water table! If children were given warm, soapy water and scrub brushes, they could clean the tables and chairs themselves. Montessori claimed that the sense of competence children gain from involvement in such real-life work is extremely beneficial and enhances children's self-esteem in a way that artificial or contrived activities never could.

Schedule Large Blocks of Open-Ended Time

Montessori's observations led her to believe that children are capable of great concentration when they are surrounded by many interesting things to do and given the time and freedom to do them. She thought that when teachers allow children to choose what they will do and how and when they will do it, the teachers have more time to observe and assist children individually. Today in US early childhood programs, children are often called to circle time or story time when they are deeply engaged in a project of their own. Teachers say they have so much to teach the children in a short amount of time that they are unable to leave the children to their own interests as much as they would like. Some teachers feel that they aren't "teaching" unless they have planned all the activities. They use plan books in which blocks of time are reserved for writing, stories, music, manipulatives, math games, and snack. Many teachers are afraid to set plan books aside. They may even call reluctant children indoors on a beautiful sunny day because "movement with silk scarves" is on the schedule.

Montessori teachers, on the other hand, are trained differently. "With my methods," writes Montessori (1912, 173), "the teacher teaches little and observes much." Teachers, of course, must plan activities and have materials on hand to support the children's interests, as suggested by Dewey's ideas in chapter 1. However, it is important to recognize the difference between the aimless activity Dewey spoke out against and purposeful, self-directed activity. When children are engaged in serious work and learning, they are not as likely to be disruptive. Montessori's theory about young children tells teachers not to pull children away from projects that interest them unless it's absolutely necessary.

Montessori believed that the only way to know how to schedule the day and manage behavior is through observation. This is why large blocks of uninterrupted time are so important to both teachers and children in early childhood classrooms. The following example, about two teachers working in the same kindergarten program but in separate classrooms, illustrates the difference observation can make to scheduling.

Janet believes that keeping consistent schedules is important for the children. Every weekend, she plans carefully for the coming week. She tries to balance indoor with outdoor time, active with quiet activities, and child-choice with teacher-directed activities. She keeps individual needs in mind. Once the plan is established, she is hesitant to change it. She believes the children are calmed by their consistent routines.

Down the hall, Bonnie works with the same age group. She and Janet agree philosophically about what is important for young children. Bonnie admits that she doesn't spend as much time planning as Janet does. She relies more heavily on constant, ongoing observation of the children. She claims she wouldn't know how to pace her days without carefully watching the children for signs of interest, fatigue, and needs.

Chapter 3

Let's look at how these two teachers manage one simple part of their day: outdoor time. Janet frequently struggles with it. She and her assistant, Laura, find that five or six of their class of eighteen are always too cold or too hot or otherwise unhappy about being outdoors. The two teachers' ability to focus on the children who are invigorated by being outdoors is diminished by the energy spent preventing negative feelings in the five or six stragglers. Once they are indoors again, Janet and Laura's energy is consumed by trying to reel in the children who need a longer period of outdoor play.

Bonnie and her assistant, Mark, have found a different way. When possible, they offer children choices about how long they spend outdoors. When Bonnie and Mark observe that five or six children are getting tired, one of them takes the small group indoors. Their careful observation and flexibility allow both scheduling and behavior management to go more smoothly.

Observation

Since Montessori trained as a doctor, when she turned her energies toward the education of young children, it seemed only natural to use her scientific skills in the classroom. She believed that if you are going to teach, you need to know all you can about those you hope to educate. She believed the way to get to know children was to watch them. Careful observation, to Montessori, was the key to determining what the children were interested in or needed to learn. She believed all children could learn. She was convinced that if children were not learning, adults were not listening carefully enough or watching closely enough. Careful observation is part of her legacy. Take time for careful observation and reflection and use these observations to guide your environment and curriculum planning.

Many early childhood programs don't take time for careful observation and reflection. "We are too busy," some teachers say. And in the same conversation, one might hear, "What can we do about these kids? They don't listen. They don't focus. There is too much running around and hitting in this classroom. How can I do observations when these kids have such demanding needs? I can't fit it in!" Montessori suggested that if we watch children carefully and then reflect on those observations, we can figure out what the children need that they are not presently getting from the environment.

I remember, for example, observing in a classroom where children's physical aggression was taking much of the teachers' time. I noticed that they were using a wonderful woodworking bench as a science table. "Do you have tools?" I asked.

Both teachers rolled their eyes and said, "Look around this room. These children don't go five minutes without hurting each other. Are you suggesting we should hand an already out-of-control group of children a bunch of hammers? Then we would really have problems!"

I asked why they thought the children acted this way. The teachers said they thought the children were not interested in doing any activities.

"Are there times when they are not as aggressive?" I asked. The teachers said that when they walked to the park, the children were able to run and climb and did not use their physical energy on each other. I asked the teachers if they would be willing to try putting out the tools to see what would happen. They agreed.

Both teachers were surprised at the outcome. The children became very involved with the hammers and nails. The children started hammering just for the sake of pounding nails and stopped hitting each other. The teachers had a little respite and were able to talk with each other about how to do more with the children's obvious need for physical release. Montessori viewed observation in this way—as a jumping-off point that helps teachers know what children need and want to be doing.

The teachers described in this story learned something new from their observations: The children needed more physical activity. They also learned that the activities offered previously had not captivated the children. The children's high energy level and the lack of solid curriculum to engage that energy had resulted in challenging behaviors. After considerable discussion and reflection on these observations, the teachers decided they needed to change the physical environment as well as the curriculum. They put some furnishings in storage and provided more space for gross-motor activities. They went to a workshop on movement and started experimenting more creatively with different kinds of music in the classroom. They increased the use of jazz and rock for children's dance experiences. The more the children moved, the less physical aggression occurred.

Initially these teachers were not convinced of Montessori's premise that observing children can give teachers clues about their curriculum needs. They were working hard to provide appropriate activities and experiences, but their ideas came from curriculum manuals, not from the children. Allowing children to provide the ideas for curriculum made their classroom a more peaceful and more exciting place to be.

These teachers learned that observing can show teachers a great deal about what children need. Unfortunately, after all the progress made in the United States in terms of developmentally appropriate practices, many early educators report that in their programs they no longer have time or permission to let children play or pursue their own interests. Some kindergarten children no longer have outdoor playtime. This may feel discouraging; trends seem to be moving backward, not forward. This is a time when it's essential to know the theoretical foundations of our discipline—so we can give good reasons why we do what we do with children when challenged by well-intentioned parents, administrators, or school board members.

Montessori had strong feelings about the tendency of adults to undermine children's competence by doing too much for them. She used the word *serve* in her discussions about this. She cautioned teachers that children remain incompetent if adults do for them what they are capable of doing themselves (Montessori 1912). Today we see a frightening return to this kind of thinking. Teachers frequently complain to me of parents who carry their five-year-olds because they are in a hurry. We often see overwhelmed and tired parents at the end of the day who are trying to carry not only their child but also their lunch box, backpack, and teddy bear out to the car, rather than asking the five-year-old to walk and carry half of the equipment. Walking is a basic skill for those of us without mobility-related disabilities, but this is a good example of a twenty-first century tendency to spare children (usually middle-class children) any effort, inconvenience, or stress. In his book *Between Parent and Teenager*, Haim Ginott (1969) likened the behavior of overly watchful parents to a helicopter hovering over their children. Helicopter parenting is still an issue, echoing Montessori's concerns of a century earlier (Sood and Buchanan 2024). Parents who solve problems for their children and are hyperinvolved in their activities can actually hold back their growth and development.

In the early 2000s, Diana West went so far as to warn that this tendency is a threat to Western civilization. Her 2007 book *The Death of the Grown-Up: How America's Arrested Development Is Bringing Down Western Civilization*, remains an important read for concerned parents and teachers. In it she describes the ways in which many thirty-year-olds in the United States are still functional adolescents. It is a frightening trend that continues as "parents accompany their teenage children to university interviews, engage directly with tutors about academic progress, or even intervene in their child's job applications and workplace matters" (Sharma and Narula 2024, 2). Over a century ago, Montessori urged teachers to organize environments for children and then make the time for children to manage on their own, and young children today need teachers who will heed this warning and stand up for children's right to do all that they are capable of doing. This does not mean we can't tie shoes or help with a jacket when a child who can do it independently is tired or irritable. It does mean that there is a well-documented trend in which

Chapter 3

adults deprive children of the satisfaction and competence that independence nurtures. Montessori's legacy is as important today as it was when she first shared her brilliant understanding of the needs of young children.

Discussion Questions

1. Last week you had a big cleaning day in your program. The children took their chairs and toys outdoors and scrubbed them down with soapy water and brushes. Today a dad complained that he does not pay tuition for his children to do your cleaning. Basing your response on Montessori's ideas about real work and responsibility, what would you say?

2. How would you use Montessori's ideas to approach the idea of early literacy in preschool programs? What materials and equipment would you use in the classroom, and what activities would you plan? Describe how Montessori's theory supports your plan.

3. Your coteacher has complained that plants take up too much space in the classroom and create additional work. You suggest that the children take over all responsibility for the plants. He complains that this would be wasting their valuable time. Using Montessori's ideas on independence and environment, how could you convince your coteacher that plant care is a good use of the children's time?

Suggestions for Further Reading

De Stefano, Cristina. 2023. *The Child Is the Teacher: A Life of Maria Montessori*. Translated by Gregory Conti. Other Press.

Hainstock, Elizabeth G. 1997. *The Essential Montessori: An Introduction to the Woman, the Writings, the Method, and the Movement*. Revised and updated ed. Plume.

Lillard, Angeline Stoll. 2005. *Montessori: The Science Behind the Genius*. Oxford University Press.

Montessori, Maria. 1965. *Dr. Montessori's Own Handbook: A Short Guide to Her Ideas and Materials*. Schocken Books.

Chapter 4: Erik Erikson

There is in every child at every stage a new miracle of vigorous unfolding, which constitutes a new hope and a new responsibility for all.

—Erik Erikson, *Childhood and Society*

Biography

ERIK ERIKSON WAS BORN in Frankfurt, Germany, in 1902. He was an artist and teacher who became interested in psychology when he met Anna Freud. Freud was a psychoanalyst and the daughter of Sigmund Freud. She convinced Erikson to study at the Vienna Psychoanalytic Institute, where he specialized in child psychoanalysis.

He came to the United States in 1933, where he joined the faculty of Harvard Medical School. Later he moved to Yale University, where he became interested in the influence of culture and society on child development. His first book, *Childhood and Society*, published in 1950, is considered a classic by educators, psychologists, and sociologists.

Erikson's later years were devoted to exploring the ways adults can continue to live meaningful and productive lives in their old age. He continued to work on development issues until he died at the age of ninety-two in 1994.

Erikson's Theories

Erikson's work has importance for every early childhood educator because it shows how children develop the foundation for emotional

Chapter 4

and social development and mental health. Erikson's theory, which is called the Eight Ages of Man, covers the entire life span of a human being. Erikson theorized that a person must accomplish a particular task at each stage of development. The resolution of each stage affects the next stage. As people pass through each stage, they form personality strengths or weaknesses based on their development during that stage. Describing this, Erikson gave us the term *identity crisis*. He considered it inevitable that young people experience conflict as they grow and change into adults.

The following chart illustrates each age, names it as a stage, and lists its strength, which is the ideal result of the developmental struggle concluded at that stage. In *Childhood and Society*, Erikson also discusses the weaknesses resulting from failure to resolve each struggle.

Erikson's Stages of Psychosocial Development		
Age	**Stage**	**Strength Developed**
Birth to 12 months	Trust vs. Mistrust	Hope
1–3 years	Autonomy vs. Shame and Doubt	Willpower
3–6 years	Initiative vs. Guilt	Purpose
6–11 years	Industry vs. Inferiority	Competence
Adolescence	Identity vs. Role Confusion	Fidelity
Young adulthood	Intimacy vs. Isolation	Love
Middle age	Generativity vs. Self-Absorption	Care
Old age	Integrity vs. Despair	Wisdom

(Erikson [1950] 1963)

Erikson was convinced that in the earliest years of life, patterns develop that regulate, or at least influence, a person's actions and interactions for the rest of their life. However, he also wrote, "There are, therefore . . . few frustrations in this or the following stages which the growing child cannot endure if the frustration leads to the ever-renewed experience of greater sameness and stronger continuity of development, toward a final integration of the individual life cycle with some meaningful wider belongingness" (Erikson [1950] 1963, 249). He believed it was always possible to go back and renegotiate issues from a previous stage of development. He was convinced that the tasks of each stage continue to present themselves at times of crisis in love and work throughout our lives. Though it is true that basic trust and independence are formed early and affect later actions and attributes, it is also true that people can choose to work toward a better resolution of any of these developmental tasks at any time throughout their lives. Erikson felt that the early childhood years were critical in children's development of trust, autonomy, and initiative, but he did not believe all was lost if children experienced difficulties in the first three stages.

Current research on early brain development, however, has challenged Erikson's belief that developmental tasks not resolved during the first three stages could be revisited and solved at a later point in time. The research shows that there are critical windows of opportunity, or developmental timetables, that signify when the brain is most fertile for specific types of learning. For example, the window of opportunity for Erikson's Trust vs. Mistrust stage is associated with the first twelve months of life. Experiences that occur within these twelve months determine whether a baby will "wire" for trust or mistrust. If a baby's needs are regularly met, the baby will wire for trust. However, if a baby's needs are not regularly met, the baby is likely to wire for mistrust. And the further a baby grows from the window of opportunity, the less chance of repair—the less likely issues from this stage of development can be learned. As researcher Mônica Scattolin summarizes,

Chapter 4

> To reach their full potential, children need to experience the five interrelated and indivisible components of nurturing care: good health, adequate nutrition, safety and security, responsive caregiving, and opportunities for learning. Nurturing care may reduce the detrimental effects of social disadvantage on brain structure and function which, in turn, improves children's health and development. . . . It has been well established that . . . a secure attachment with caretakers improves the capacity of emotional connectivity, the ability to build safe and secure relationships, and the development of positive self-esteem later in life. (Scattolin et al. 2022)

Erikson's first three stages will be discussed here, since these are the stages that affect children in early childhood.

Trust Versus Mistrust

Erikson's first stage of psychosocial development, which takes place during the baby's first year of life, is trust versus mistrust. Babies' task during this time is to develop a sense of trust in themselves, in other people, and in the world around them. Erikson wrote about trust as having two parts, external (belief that significant adults will be present to meet the baby's needs) and internal (belief in their own power to effect change and cope with a variety of circumstances). Babies who successfully adapt during this first stage approach the second year of life with a sure sense that the world is a good place to be. They believe that adults will be there to meet their material needs and to guide and support them. They trust that adults will lend stability and continuity of care to their lives. They know they have the power to engage adults (through tears, smiles, or fussing) whenever they need help.

This engaging of adults is part of what educators call attachment. It is a special bond between babies and the significant adults in their lives. When the baby is in the presence of these adults, their sense of security and comfort is heightened. The baby uses them as a safe place from which to go out and explore the world. When babies encounter a threat of any kind (unusual sights, sounds, or situations), they need to be able to return quickly to the arms of a trusted adult for comfort and reassurance. When babies develop a strong sense of trust during their first year, they become attached to the important people in their lives. However, whenever one ponders the parents who are committed to "attachment parenting" (Sears and Sears 2001), which advises parents to be baby-centered and not parent-centered, Erikson's theory of internal trust comes to mind. If we race in at every indication of distress, how will the baby know they can cope with anything?

Erikson believed that accomplishment of each developmental stage lays the foundation for the next stage. A basic sense of trust is necessary for children to move into the next stage and develop autonomy. For example, a common characteristic of children who lack strong attachments with important adults is the failure to develop empathy (the ability to put yourself in another person's place and understand how they feel). In recent years, when juveniles have committed violent crimes and express no remorse, headlines have asked, "Why?" The answer, of course, is far more complex than Erikson's theory of emotional development. Yet some of his writing from decades ago seems prophetic, in light of the state of many children in the United States today. When children's needs go unmet, they are unable to develop trust in themselves or the world around them. According to Erikson, children lacking this basic sense of trust are incapable of developing higher levels of social functioning.

Erikson believed that two actions on the part of parents and teachers help babies develop this basic sense of trust:

- holding babies close and having warm physical contact with them when they are being fed
- responding right away to their distress when they cry or fuss

Both of these actions are critical teaching skills for infant care providers. Increasing numbers of young babies are spending their days in child care centers or in family child care. Changing social conditions do not change the developmental needs of young children. The needs of babies for predictable, loving care have not changed. Our challenge, then, is to create places where babies' needs are met and where parents' attempts to meet their babies' needs are received with a joyful, welcoming response by providers. Child care centers must provide an atmosphere in which babies and their families can thrive.

Teachers wanting to support the development of trust in infants need to

- hold babies during feedings,

- respond to signals of distress, and

- support babies' attachment through primary caregiving.

Hold Babies During Feeding
The pleasure of warmth and cuddling when being fed is as essential an ingredient for a baby's emotional development as the nutritious meal is for their physical development. At this early age, it is through feelings that a baby learns. When a familiar adult's smiling face kisses and cuddles a baby at feeding time, they learn that they are important and lovable. Once teachers know that comfort and pleasure for infants during feeding is as important as the nutrition, they can plan the program in the infant room accordingly. Soft lights, calming music, and a rocking chair set the stage for pleasant mealtimes. Building relationships during feedings requires that teachers focus on the baby—smiling, cuddling, and talking. This isn't a time for teachers to talk with each other about next week's staff meeting! Some centers post signs on the door to the infant room stating, "No interruptions; please, we are having lunch!" This gives the clear

message that phone calls, messages, and visitors (except, of course, the babies' parents) are not welcome during this special time for teachers and babies.

Since attachment to special adults is an important piece of this stage of development, arranging for the same teacher to feed the same babies as much as schedules can possibly allow will support the babies in their acquisition of that basic sense of trust.

Erikson makes it clear that a huge piece of accomplishing this first stage of development is the quality of the parent-child relationship. Babies need as much warm, loving contact with their parents as they can get. For this reason, infant programs must provide not only a welcoming attitude toward nursing but also a physical space offering privacy, quiet music, and comfortable seating where parents and babies can share a special mealtime.

Respond to Distress

In every child development course I've ever taught, someone has asked about "spoiling" children by responding to them when they cry. Once an infant provider rolled her eyes at me as she walked with a screaming baby and said, "This child is just too attached to her parents! I'm trying to teach her that we can't just come running every time she cries!"

If teachers provide care based on Erikson's theories, they accept that babies have few coping skills and that it is therefore up to adults to keep them comfortable. Programs whose staff understand infant development will have policies of quickly responding to babies' tears. In the United States, though, the notion persists that adults "spoil" babies by giving them the attention they cry for.

Erikson's theory says that babies will develop the strongest sense of security if they know that adults will come running when they cry. Then, when they are a little older, they will be able to cope with delayed gratification of their needs. By meeting babies' needs quickly and consistently throughout their first year of life, teachers are doing the opposite of spoiling. With consistent, responsive care, they are laying the foundation that will allow babies to grow into strong, confident toddlers ready to assert their independence.

It is important to note here that some of the overreaction to attachment parenting has resulted in parents never giving the child the opportunity to cope with any level of distress. Research, as well as Montessori's original work on developing independence, has stressed the importance of learning to cope (Young-Eisendrath 2008; Chang et al. 2015; Eisenberg et al. 2001). Babies whose needs are consistently met quickly can learn to cope with small amounts of distress. Parents and teachers need the confidence to let them try in small doses. It is a matter of balance.

Support Attachment Through Primary Caregiving

Erikson's theory of infant development assures teachers that it is impossible for a baby under a year of age to be "too attached" to the special adults in her life. The provider in the story above who wanted to teach the baby that adults can't always be there was missing the central point of providing high-quality care to infants. Attachment is what developing a sense of trust is all about. It is the provider's job to provide as much stability in care as possible. For this reason, organizing staff schedules in an infant center around primary caregivers is a good idea.

Erikson stressed how important it is for babies to have significant relationships with a few key adults in order to accomplish the task of developing basic trust. For these relationships to develop in child care settings, babies need to count on the same adult being there when they wake from a nap, need their diapers changed, come in from a walk, or need to be fed. Objections to primary caregiving are sometimes raised by both parents and teachers. Some teachers in infant care settings say that babies cry all day if their primary caregiver is absent from the center. Parents, too, will sometimes say, "I worry that she is too attached to her primary caregiver. Last week when the teacher was out sick, my baby cried all day."

The fact that separation from those special adults causes distress for babies and demands the comfort of others is not a good reason, according to Erikson, to try to prevent this attachment. Attachment is essential, even if it is not permanent, and the process of mourning for a special adult and being comforted by other reliable adults is another indication to babies that their needs will be met. Erikson's theory confirms that strong relationships with a few significant adults in the first year of life are important, even if babies have to separate later from the people to whom they are attached. As Alfred Tennyson's famous poem says, it's "better to have loved and lost than never to have loved at all."

Autonomy Versus Shame and Doubt

Erikson's second stage of psychosocial development, which takes place during the child's second and third year of life, is autonomy versus shame and doubt. The developmental task of this stage is to acquire a sense of autonomy (independence) without suffering extremes of shame and doubt. Children who successfully adapt during this stage of development will acquire a strong sense of self. They will be able to separate confidently, for limited periods of time, from parents and primary caregivers. They will demand to do things for themselves whenever possible. Toddler teachers become accustomed to the shouts of "No! Me! Mine! Me do it!" that are characteristic of this stage of development. Toddlers also have a way of being fiercely independent one minute and needy and clinging the next.

According to Erikson, this is all a natural part of toddler development. He said that during this second stage, children are dealing with the challenges of holding on and letting go. Erikson meant several things by this. He knew that both holding on and letting go can be positive and negative forces in human behavior. Holding on can be destructive: controlling, unyielding, and uncooperative behaviors. Holding on can also be constructive: attachment to special people, courage in the face of adversity, or plain old persistence in getting a task done. Letting go can be destructive: tantrums, losing control when angry, hitting, or biting. Letting go can also be constructive: cooperating in relationships, sharing, or yielding to the plans of others. Again, it is a matter of balance.

Erikson believed that toddlers struggle to achieve balance between appropriate holding on and letting go. Areas for these struggles include sharing with friends, relationships with parents and primary caregivers, independent toileting, and making choices. Erikson thought that one of the main barriers for toddlers in accomplishing this task is overcontrolling behavior from adults who thwart and resist the toddlers' growing demands for independence. When adults are unable to adjust to a child's swinging between needs for dependence and independence at this stage, they often shame the child for behavior that is actually developmentally appropriate. For children, the effects of this shaming response are twofold. In the short term, the toddler becomes even more frustrated and resistant. In the long term, the child models the adult behavior, becoming controlling and unyielding. To develop a strong sense of independence, toddlers need to have reasonable opportunities for choice and control. At the same time, they need consistent, firm, reassuring limits set by caring adults. Toddlers can easily be victims of their own strong feelings and sometimes do need us to step in. It is our responsibility to do so.

Erikson said that this stage is an important time in development because its outcomes largely determine the ratio of love and hate, cooperation or lack of it, and freedom of expression or tendency to suppress feelings that become part of who we are for the rest of our lives. When children can fully develop a strong sense of self-control without loss of self-esteem, they will feel proud and confident. When children experience loss of control and excessive shame, they will tend to doubt themselves. Again, in light of the more current studies cited above, adequate, not excessive, self-esteem is our goal for positive emotional health.

It is clear that toddler caregivers have a balancing act on their hands as they guide young children throughout this tumultuous stage. Erikson believed that with the support and understanding of significant adults, toddlers can navigate this stage, emerging confident and ready to take the initiative in their next stage of development. Erikson believed that adults can foster independence in children of this age by

- giving children simple choices,
- not giving false choices,
- setting clear, consistent, reasonable limits, and
- accepting children's swings between independence and dependence and reassuring them that both are okay.

Erikson believed that children need to be able to experience the fury and demands of this unpredictable stage of their development without losing the support and reassurance of the important adults in their lives. If adults provide choices and clear limits, toddlers can thrive and feel comfortable with their need to be a "big kid" one minute and a "baby" the next.

Give Children Simple Choices

According to Erikson, toddlers need to experience the independence of being able to make some choices for themselves. Toddler programs can support their independence by arranging for self-selection of activities and materials. Rooms should include low shelves for equipment where toddlers can make their choices without help from others. There should be duplicates or multiple copies of favorite toys and books, since sharing is not yet a well-developed skill. This makes life easier for teachers and happier for toddlers, since it reduces territorial toddler conflict.

Schedules should include lots of time in which toddlers can choose what they want to do from a range of acceptable options.

Teachers should avoid expecting all the children to do the same thing at the same time. Teachers can support toddlers in making reasonable choices for themselves and expressing their preferences, even when it's not possible to do exactly what the children would like to do at that moment. Teachers can acknowledge their feelings with phrases such as this: "I know, you want to go outside right now. I wish we could go out too. We can go out when all the diapers are changed."

Choices need to be simple at this age to help children learn how to choose and to keep the alternatives manageable for teachers. Most two-year-olds aren't ready for "What would you like for lunch today?" But choosing between a cheese sandwich and a peanut butter sandwich offers just the right challenge. Looking at a drawer full of clothing might reduce a toddler to tears or a tantrum because the choices are so overwhelming. Choosing between a red shirt and a yellow shirt offers a toddler enough independence to feel they have control over their life.

Eliminate False Choices

Many teachers make the mistake of offering toddlers a choice when there really isn't one. For a child who is trying to learn how much control they really have, it's confusing to be asked a rhetorical question. Adults and school-age children can understand that "Would you like to do the dishes?" is a request or a politely phrased expectation. Toddlers cannot distinguish between this kind of question and a real choice. For this reason, teachers are sometimes surprised when they ask, "Would you like to go out to play now?" and the child who thought they had a choice wails at being thrust into their jacket against their will.

To offer children in this stage the control they need, try phrasing necessary changes in a way that offers a choice of *how* (not *whether*) the task will be accomplished. For example, state, "We are going out now. Would you like me to help you put on your jacket, or do you want to do it yourself?" This makes it clear that the doing (going out, coming in, taking a nap, and so on) is not a choice. The choice is whether the child gets ready independently or receives some adult help.

Set Clear Limits

Erikson believed that a toddler struggles greatly between inner and outer control. Toddlers are working on their sense of self. Their sense of others is still primitive. They will push, hit, bite, and throw things in a most matter-of-fact way. For this reason, teachers do toddlers a service by setting clear, firm limits. When outer limits are clear, children can focus on learning inner control. When outer limits are inconsistent or poorly stated, children must continually put energy into finding out what the limits are.

This is an area where I have observed less teacher competence in the new millennium than previously. Stating limits clearly is essential to helping toddlers meet their own needs. Working on teacher talk that is not confusing will help teachers with this stage. I discuss this topic at length in my book *Choose Your Words: Communicating with Young Children* (Redleaf Press, 2018).

Accept Alternating Needs for Independence and Dependence

When toddlers strive for independence, they do it with passion. Their insistence on having things their way can be downright defiant! According to Erikson, for children to have their own way at this stage is critical to healthy development. Unless children are putting themselves or others in danger, toddler teachers need to support their drive to do something their own way. Teachers should yield to children's need to be held and rocked and also to their fierce need to do things for themselves. When teachers understand that this seesaw behavior is a normal part of toddler development, it is easier to cope with the variety of moods and behaviors a toddler presents in a short period of time. Teachers' acceptance of these changing moods helps toddlers grow in confidence and self-esteem.

Again, the culture in the United States today calls for some adaptation to our approach to toddler tantrums. It is probably fair to say that decades ago, both parents and teachers were not tolerant enough, but today's parents and teachers are at risk of tolerating too much.

Toddlers' constantly changing needs for dependence and independence can be supported in the environment as well. Easels, water tables, and dramatic play materials are as important to toddlers as they are to preschoolers. Soft toys, board books, and push/pull toys are as important here as in environments for younger babies. An approach to environment that includes both offers comfort to children as they engage alternately in "big kid" and "baby" behaviors throughout their toddler days.

Initiative Versus Guilt

The third and last stage of Erikson's theory that addresses the early childhood years is initiative versus guilt. Most four- and five-year-olds are at this stage, so it's a key one for preschool and kindergarten teachers to know about. The developmental task of this stage is to acquire a sense of purpose.

Erikson describes children of this age as energetic and ready to learn. Typically developing children will forget failures more quickly by age four or five. They are more willing to listen and learn from teachers, parents, and other children. At this stage children are growing in ways that make them much more actively focused and less defiant. Children who have negotiated their second stage successfully have established their autonomy, so they act less for the sake of individual control and more to get things done. Children who successfully accomplish the developmental tasks of this stage will emerge confident and competent. They will believe that they can plan and complete a task independently. They will be able to cope with and learn from mistakes without feeling guilty about things that don't go as planned.

At first glance, this stage seems much easier for adults than the previous two. This is partly due to the child's growing cognitive and physical abilities. The developmental task does not require as much energy from adults. In addition, it involves less of the aggressive behavior characteristic of toddler development. According to Erikson, however, this third stage is a time when the child's development can split in one of two possible directions: If we encourage preschool children to use their energy in an active and involved way, their confidence will grow. Their competence will increase. But if we do for them what they can do for themselves, or if we focus on the mistakes they make on the way to developing new skills, their sense of initiative can turn to guilt and discouragement. There seems to be less tendency today to focus on children's mistakes in a negative way. However, there is a documented trend of parents consistently doing for children what they are capable of doing themselves.

Of course, most teachers don't purposely focus on children's mistakes instead of their successes. However, according to Erikson, when teachers hover near the easel, wiping up each drop of paint that goes astray, children are likely to feel less competent and take fewer risks in learning. I once observed a teacher who was great with insects, farm units, and birds. But whenever the children played with water or dirt, she was visibly unsettled. I watched her one morning sweeping up sand as soon as it fell from the sand table. She hovered around the water table with towels, wiping up every drop that hit the floor. She always smiled at the children. She never said, "Careful! Careful! Don't spill the water! Don't let the sand fall!" Her constant vigilance, however, gave off a strong message of intolerance. The children in this room did not use the sand and water tables much. It wasn't possible for them to feel competent there in the face of this teacher's behavior.

When children are subjected to expectations beyond their abilities during this stage, they have no way of knowing that adult goals for them are inappropriate. They may respond to this situation in either of two ways: They may decide subconsciously that they are not capable and give up on the task. Or they may push themselves beyond their capabilities and succeed against the odds. These children mind all the rules, meet all the expectations, and seem to manage just fine. You might ask, "What's wrong with this? Is there really a problem with overachievers or diligent workers?" The problem is that often these children learn that their value is measured by *what* they do rather than by *who* they are. Their initiative has not been damaged, but they still may carry a heavy load of feelings of guilt and inadequacy. They pay an emotional price for their success at adapting to unreasonable expectations.

Judith Warner's 2005 book *Perfect Madness: Motherhood in the Age of Anxiety* sounded the alarm on the pressure contemporary middle-class parents experience in the United States to "help" their children succeed in an overly competitive academic and social arena. In today's world, helicopter parents continue to place unreasonable expectations on their very young children (Vigdal and Brønnick 2022), compounding them by doing the homework or "helping" rather than letting the child develop at their own pace. According to both Erikson's theory and more contemporary writers, this is a recipe for disaster.

To support children's development of initiative in the third stage, Erikson says that teachers can do the following:

- encourage children to be as independent as possible
- focus on gains as children practice new skills, not on the mistakes they make along the way
- set expectations that are in line with children's individual abilities
- focus curriculum on real things and on doing

Encourage Independence

Teachers who apply Erikson's understanding of young children's development to their daily work with children will create classrooms where children can do things for themselves. Materials and equipment will be easily accessible to children, organized in ways that make it possible for them both to find what they need and put it away when they're done. Children will know where to find pails and sponges and paper towels to clean up messes when necessary. Family-style meals offer children opportunities to serve themselves, to pour from pitchers even if they spill, and to clean up their places when they are finished.

Focus on Gains, Not Mistakes

According to Erikson, preschool children need the confident message from us that we take their initiative seriously. They need to know that their work is far more important than their messes or their mistakes.

For example, one year I observed a teacher named Susan who often said to the children she taught, "Life is a work in progress!" She understood that sometimes children need a place to set a project for a while until they decide to come back to it. She encouraged the children to write stories, and her five-year-old students knew what an editor was. They were not afraid to make mistakes because, after all, these were only drafts. Susan sometimes asked the other adults in the room how to spell a word, or what ten times eleven was, modeling that teachers don't know everything, need help from others, forget things, and make mistakes. She was quick to show the children the things she had learned by making mistakes. One day I heard her say confidently to the children, "I'm getting better at the computer. I practice every day. I notice that I don't make mistakes as often as I used to."

This kind of teaching, according to Erikson, supports children's sense of competence in learning and contributes to their development of a sense of purpose.

Chapter 4

Consider Individual Differences

Teachers work hard to plan curriculum appropriate to the ages of children they teach. But often it's easy to forget the day-to-day differences that children bring with them. For example, if four-year-old Ana has a new baby brother at home, cooperating with others in a typically age-appropriate way might be too big a challenge for her right now. If the teacher expects Ana to share her new book even though she has recently had to share her parents for the first time, Ana is vulnerable to discouragement or guilt. Aware of Erikson's theory about children's development, the teacher might say, "Usually I would ask Ana to share that with the class, but today I think she needs to have it all to herself." This approach shows the understanding that, according to Erikson, teachers must consider not only children's developmental stage, but also the individual factors that control what they are capable of on any given day.

It is harder and harder to focus on individual differences as expected skills are pushed aggressively at earlier and earlier ages. It is, however, probably more important than ever that we heed Erikson's warning to do so.

Focus Curriculum on Real Things

Erikson believed that children in the stage of initiative versus guilt need real tools and real tasks in order to develop their competence. For example, Marcus planned to make vegetable soup with his preschoolers. When the cook brought him butter knives for the children to use to chop vegetables, he explained that if the children tried to cut carrots and celery with butter knives, they would fail. Instead, he taught them how to use sharp knives carefully. The children did a great job cutting the vegetables with the sharp knives. They also experienced a boost in confidence as they demonstrated how capable they really were.

For the same reasons, it makes just as much sense to teachers who understand Erikson to use real tools in the woodworking area.

When children are carefully taught how to care for the tools and how to use them safely, their sense of competence skyrockets.

Erikson in the Twenty-First Century

Erikson was able to develop his stages from almost a purely psychosocial perspective, writing decades before brain imaging and similar types of scientific research were even possible. But our growing knowledge regarding brain development and windows of opportunity for growth has serious implications for practice. Additionally, it is impossible today to contemplate psychosocial development without focusing on culture, community, health and wellness, and changing family structures. This is not to say that Erikson's work is now out of date and not helpful to our understanding of young children's emotional development. But it means that we must apply that broader lens when we view the many variables involved.

When Erikson did his foundational studies on stages of development, there was little in the way of sympathetic understanding of young children. He reminded us that infant trust begins when adults respond quickly to infant tears. He urged parents to understand that two-year-olds needed to assert their independence, and this would sometimes result in meltdowns. It was a time when Benjamin Spock was warning parents about their child ruling the home if strict measures were not taken. It was a time when parents of six-year-olds were excited when their children learned the ABCs in first grade—and no one still in diapers played the violin or took swimming lessons.

So once again we need to exercise caution and balance as we look at educational psychology and daily practices. Perhaps the newest piece of this puzzle is the growing body of knowledge about how extreme some of our practices with young children have become. Here I am referring to the changes observed by Polly Young-Eisendrath (2008) and others of parents striving to develop positive self-esteem at any cost, of children running many homes in the

Chapter 4

United States rather than the parents, and of educational standards taking a direction that well-trained educators know is contrary to healthy development of young children. For some of you, the reference above stating that seventy years ago both parents and teachers were thrilled if first graders had learned their ABCs might be startling. If you do not work with young children on a daily basis, you may be surprised to see young children who frequently boss their parents around at the end of the day in child care. They say where they will go for dinner and who will come for a playdate this weekend. Too frequently those of us who do work every day with young children see parents give in to these demands.

Young families today live in more social isolation than most families in this country did in the early twentieth century. With both parents employed all day and US parental leave policies being practically nonexistent, most parents don't have the opportunity to observe and live with their child all day long for more than a few weeks. This reality does not cultivate feelings of competence as a parent. Teacher education programs for early educators need to increase the "family support" component of their curricula. We need to demand that schools focus on the developmental needs and the individual needs of young children and that developmentally appropriate practice in the early years be respected. For this reason, those of us who work in the field must stay abreast of the changes in society and pedagogy that affect our work. We must review the theoretical foundations of our discipline so we have the appropriate reasons and justification for individualized instruction, outdoor play, and other important pieces of children's growth and development that are at risk in modern US culture.

Discussion Questions

1. Sydney is twelve weeks old. The teacher who usually cares for her is out sick. Sydney cries and cries. When her mom picks her up at child care, she is upset that Sydney is exhausted and

fretful. She requests that Sydney have several providers rather than a primary caregiver because she does not want more long, hard days like today. What do you say? How is this related to Erikson's theories?

2. At a parent meeting, Samuel's dad complains that he was "well-behaved" when he was in the infant room. Now that he has moved to the toddler room, he is always shouting "No!" and running away. He pushed his eighteen-month-old cousin this weekend and grabbed his truck, yelling "Mine!" Samuel's dad wants to know when you will teach these children to share and behave. What will you say? How can Erikson's theory of autonomy help you answer the question?

3. Madison is in your kindergarten class. So is her best friend, Ella. When Ella's grandma dies, you read *Nana Upstairs and Nana Downstairs* by Tomie dePaola. The children talk a bit about dying. Later in the week, Madison's mom comes in angry. She says these discussions have no place at school. She does not want Madison upset. "She is just now getting over the death of my grandmother!" she says. You know that Madison's great-grandmother was special to them because she raised Madison's mom. You assure her that Madison has shown no sign of stress, but her mom is still upset. What do you think this is about? What does it have to do with Erikson's theories? How can you help?

Suggestions for Further Reading

Coles, Robert, ed. 2000. *The Erik Erikson Reader.* W. W. Norton & Company.

Erikson, H. Erik. 1968. *Identity: Youth and Crisis.* W. W. Norton & Company.

Chapter 4

Sousa, David A. 2006. *How the Brain Learns*. 3rd ed. Corwin Press.

Warner, Judith. 2005. *Perfect Madness: Motherhood in the Age of Anxiety*. Riverhead Books.

Chapter 5: Jean Piaget

The teacher-organizer should know not only his own science but also be well versed in the details of the development of the child's or adolescent's mind.

—**Jean Piaget,** *To Understand Is to Invent*

Biography

JEAN PIAGET WAS BORN in Neuchâtel, Switzerland, in 1896. He was a budding scientist at an early age, publishing a scholarly paper at the age of eleven. Throughout his long career, he added more than sixty books and hundreds of articles to his accomplishments. Although Piaget is frequently referred to as a psychologist, he was really an epistemologist (someone who studies the nature and beginning of knowledge). It is this piece of his work that has made Piaget a major contributor to educational psychology. While others asked *what* children know or *when* they know it, Piaget asked *how* children arrive at what they know.

Like many of us, Piaget hadn't planned on a career of working with children. He received a doctorate in biology but never worked in that field. Instead, he turned to psychology. In 1919 Piaget traveled to Paris to study and took a job at the Alfred Binet Laboratory School. His job was to standardize the French version of a British intelligence test. While doing this work, Piaget began to notice similarities in the wrong answers children gave to questions at certain ages, and he began to wonder what thought processes they were using. This became the research question that would drive his life's work. He continued to pursue his interest in children and their thought processes until his death in 1980.

Piaget's work has been a primary influence in US preschool programs since the 1970s. The volumes of Piaget's work provide an in-depth view of how children create knowledge. Unfortunately, much of his work is difficult to read and can be intimidating to busy teachers. In addition, Piaget's work has been criticized in recent years for limitations that have been challenged by current research. Specifically, many teachers think he focused too much on thought processes and not enough on children's feelings and social relationships with teachers and peers. Many also believe his use of unfamiliar terminology confuses the reader. In addition, because much of his observation was done on his own three children, critics say the work is not scientific research.

Nonetheless, Piaget's stages of cognitive development have created our overall view of how children think in their early years, just as Erikson's stages of emotional and social development have helped us understand how children develop emotionally. We can accept that while some of Piaget's theories are not as true of young children as we once thought, his basic concepts still help us plan curriculum to challenge young children's minds. To dismiss his work because of its flaws would be a mistake. The most sensible words I've read about Piaget's contributions come from Elizabeth Jones (1986, 99–100), who says,

> People in all times and places invent explanations for what happens to them, and all explanations have predictive power; they enable us to say, "See, I told you." In our culture we call our explanations science and pretend they're real, not invented. But scientific explanations change, just as myths and superstitions do, because even in physics, and certainly in psychology, they provide only partial explanations of the way things really happen. Learn them, use them, but don't take them too seriously. Nothing happens because Piaget says it does. Piaget

says it does because it happens, and he was an unusually thoughtful observer and generalizer. All of us can grow in our ability to do the same.

Piaget's Theories

While others of his time argued that learning is either intrinsic (coming from the child) or extrinsic (imposed by the environment or taught by adults), Piaget thought that neither position by itself explains learning, but that the child's interactions with the environment are what create learning. He claimed that children construct their own knowledge by giving meaning to the people, places, and things in their world. He was fond of the expression "construction is superior to instruction" (Hendrick 1992, 476). By this he meant that children learn best when they are actually doing the work themselves and creating their own understanding of what's going on, instead of being given explanations by adults. He was a student of Montessori's work and built on her idea that meaningful work is important to children's cognitive development. Like Montessori, Piaget believed children need every possible opportunity to do things for themselves. For example, children might be interested in how things grow. If a teacher reads them a finely illustrated book on how things grow, this instruction will increase their knowledge. But if the children plant a garden at school, the process of digging, watering, observing, and experiencing growing things will help them construct a knowledge of growing things that they cannot ever achieve merely by looking at pictures.

Like Dewey, Piaget believed that children learn only when their curiosity is not fully satisfied. He thought that children's curiosity drives their learning. According to Piaget, the best strategy for preschool curriculum is to keep children curious, make them wonder, and offer them real problem-solving challenges, rather than giving them information. Many adults still hold the notion that a teacher is someone who shares information. Using Piaget's theory about children's learning requires changing the image of teacher into someone who nurtures inquiry and supports the child's own search for answers.

Piaget also stressed the importance of play as an avenue for learning. As children engage in symbolic play (making a cake out of sand, using a garden hose to be a firefighter), they make sense of the objects and activities that surround them. As they imitate what goes on around them, they begin to understand how things work and what things are for. Initially this is a process of trial and error. However, with time and repetition, they use new information to increase their understanding of the world around them.

Piaget believed that children all pass through the same stages when developing their thinking skills. The age at which children accomplish these stages of development can vary. Because of this variation, charts outlining Piaget's stages may also differ slightly. Parents and teachers should always remember that individual children have their own rates of development. Differences in development stretch over a broad continuum. For example, many books cite ten to thirteen months as a typical age range for first steps. Yet walking as early as eight months or as late as eighteen months is still within the range of typical development.

Many teachers and other adults wonder if there are things that prevent growth or if there are ways to hurry development along. Piaget believed that children's intellectual growth is based partly on physical development. He also believed that it is affected by children's interactions with the environment. He did not believe that teachers can "teach" young children to understand a concept. He was certain that children build their own understanding of the world by the things they do.

According to Piaget, children's cognitive development passes through the stages shown in the chart below. What follows is a basic discussion of Piaget's first two stages in children's journey to build knowledge, since these are the stages that most concern teachers in early care and education settings.

Piaget's Stages of Cognitive Development		
Age	Stage	Behaviors
Birth to age 2	Sensorimotor	Learn through the senses; learn through reflexes; manipulate materials.
2–7 years	Preoperational	Form ideas based on their perceptions; can only focus on one variable at a time; overgeneralize based on limited experience.
7–11 or 12 years	Concrete Operational	Form ideas based on reasoning; limit thinking to objects and familiar events.
11 or 12 years and older	Formal Operational	Think conceptually; think hypothetically.

(Piaget 1973)

The Sensorimotor Stage

Piaget believed that in the beginning, babies' reactions to the world are purely reflexive (without thought). He said that intelligence begins when the reactions become purposeful. For example, when we watch an infant lying below a crib gym, we notice that initially they show a startled response if their hand or foot hits a bell or rattle, but that over time they hit the bell on purpose. This first stage of cognitive development Piaget called the sensorimotor stage. During this time, the baby relies on his senses and physical activity to learn about the world.

Toward the end of this first stage, Piaget says, object permanence occurs. Object permanence means that the baby has come to realize that something exists even when they can't see it. This is a very important development for children. Before achieving this milestone, a baby only thinks about what is in their view at the time. For

Chapter 5

example, if we carefully watch babies, we see that before eight to ten months, they drop things from their high chair tray without making a fuss. This is because for a young baby, if things are out of sight, they are literally out of mind. From the baby's point of view, they no longer exist. Then suddenly, at eight to ten months, when that spoon drops from the tray, the baby leans over, pointing and fussing and wanting it back. Often parents and providers are surprised and dismayed when they pick it up and hand it to a smiling baby—who tosses it right back down again. This is not the beginning of premeditated attempts to drive adults crazy. This is the first burst of the joy of learning! This is object permanence.

This is also the age at which we see separation anxiety in children. They cry when their parents leave them at child care or when their primary caregiver is not present. Now the baby understands that when his parent or provider is not in sight, that person is somewhere else. The caregiver hasn't just ceased to exist. So the baby makes attempts to bring that important person back into view—by crying.

To support cognitive development in children under two, Piaget's theory tells teachers to do the following:

- keep babies safe but interested
- respond reassuringly to separation anxiety

Keep Babies Safe but Interested
Since motor development is a significant learning task of the sensorimotor stage, one of the most important supports to cognitive development that infant/toddler teachers can establish is a safe and interesting environment. Babies need to push, pull, and manipulate objects. They need to crawl, climb, and pull up to standing positions without being physically at risk. An infant environment with multilevel furnishings and climbing opportunities allows babies the opportunities they need to experiment with spatial relationships

and learn through their bodies. According to Piaget, babies also need interesting things to touch and explore. A variety of cause-and-effect toys (toys that make noise when pushed, pulled, or shaken) such as crib gyms and shape sorters are essential. Babies also need to have experiences with soft materials such as nontoxic playdough, oobleck (a cornstarch-and-water mixture), water, and sand. Mirrors and artwork at babies' eye level, plus board books and cloth books that children can reach, provide even more interesting possibilities. As ECE administrator Lisa Ranfos (2024) noted, "We know that everything is a learning opportunity for [infants]. They are taking in all these sights; there's different people and different smells and all these differences, and we have to treat them as individuals."

Babies' cognitive development is also stimulated by adults who talk with them, tell them what will be happening, and delight in their accomplishments. Comfortable places for adults working in infant/toddler programs help them focus on the children and invite them to sit at the babies' level to provide another essential kind of interaction.

Respond Reassuringly to Separation Anxiety

When children are beginning to experience object permanence and thus separation anxiety, it is important to make as few changes in their lives as possible. With a little experience, they will begin to see that when people they love go away, they always return. But during the transition time, it's a good idea to keep schedules routine. For example, this is not a good time to make new child care arrangements. Providers who understand this stage can help parents see why their babies are suddenly more upset than usual when they say goodbye. They can reassure parents that this stage will pass if they can just give it a little time.

The challenges of separation anxiety have implications not only for how children are handled in the program, but for enrollment policy as well. For example, Gini was the director of a center I supervised. She told me about holding an intake interview with parents who were considering moving their child from another provider into her center. She listened sympathetically as parents described tearful separations every morning from their ten-month-old baby. The parents were certain that their child must not like his current child care arrangements but couldn't tell them that because he wasn't yet talking. Gini talked with them about separation problems and encouraged them to wait another month or two before making any changes. She suggested that the baby would probably pass through this stage and be fine. The parents thanked her and left. A week later, she heard at a directors' meeting that the baby had been taken out of his current situation and enrolled at another nearby center. She was disappointed because she knew the baby would now suffer even greater separation anxiety that probably could have been avoided if the other center's policies had supported children's developmental needs, and if the family had chosen to wait a bit.

Providers can also support parents at this stage of development by welcoming them to call at any time to see how their child is doing and by acknowledging how hard it is for parents to walk away when their child is screaming. If parents are anxious, their babies will share that anxiety, which makes things worse. Everything teachers can do to reassure parents during this stage of infant development will support the growth of the babies in their care. Some programs don't even wait for parents to contact them; they initiate the exchange because they understand how stressful it is for parents to be away from their babies. Sometimes parents get locked into a guilt reaction when their infant screams at separation in the morning. A quick message to say the baby's doing fine and to share a story about their morning often makes the day easier for parents. When parents are supported in these ways, they are better able to maintain consistent schedules for their babies, which helps the babies get through separation anxiety more quickly and successfully.

Caring for parents is a big part of supporting children's development during the earliest months of life. New parents are under stress. Some parents have anxiety because they are forced to return to work before they are ready to leave their babies. Some parents wish they could stay at home but can't afford to. Others are eager to return to work but feel guilty and conflicted about doing so. Piaget's concept of object permanence and the separation anxiety that often accompanies it is not something most young parents know about. When teachers help parents understand their children's development, they are helping parents support that development.

The Preoperational Stage

According to Piaget, after the sensorimotor stage, children's cognitive development enters the preoperational stage, which extends from the second year of life through age seven or eight. The preoperational stage is when children's thinking differs most from adult thought patterns. Piaget said that during the preoperational stage, children are egocentric (think of everything only as it relates to them), can focus on only one characteristic of a thing or a person at a time (for example, interpret words literally), gather information from what they experience rather than from what they are told, and overgeneralize from their experience.

Egocentrism means seeing the world from only one's own point of view. When observing preschoolers, adults frequently hear conversations like this one:

> Teacher: "We are having Blue Day! I've brought in many beautiful things for our blue display. We have blue paint at the easel, and I've put 'Rhapsody in Blue' in the CD player."
> Child 1: "My mom's car is blue."
> Child 2: "My mom's car is broke."
> Child 3: "My TV is broke."
> Teacher to child 1: "Your mom's car is blue?"
> Child 1: "I saw *Bluey* on TV."

These children are typical of the preoperational developmental stage. This is the egocentrism Piaget refers to. The children are not connecting with each other's stories; rather, each child's words trigger other children's thoughts about their own situations. Another familiar example of egocentrism in young children is the child who wants to buy a stuffed toy as a gift for a parent or grandparent. Because this would please the child, they believe their grandfather will also love it!

Piaget believed that in the preoperational stage, children form ideas from their direct experiences in life. This is why telling them information is less effective than helping them think their own way through a problem. For example, if a child sees birds fly away when a dog barks, they may decide that barking dogs cause birds to fly. Even though this is not an accurate conclusion, the child will be perfectly comfortable with their own reasoning despite any attempt to tell them otherwise. It is only after they have gathered more experience on their own (seeing birds take flight when no dog is around) that they will go through a mental process that challenges their worldview, a process Piaget calls disequilibrium, and adapt it to the new information. Piaget calls the process of adapting one's understanding on the basis of new information accommodation. Accommodation returns the child to a more comfortable balanced state that Piaget calls equilibrium.

Because preoperational children tend to believe what they see, they do not yet have a firm grasp of qualities belonging to the objects in their world. For example, they confuse the concept of heaviness with the concept of largeness. Due to inexperience, most young children are initially surprised that a beach ball is lighter than a baseball. Similarly, unable to separate the concept of height from that of age, preoperational children will insist that the tallest person is the oldest. Piaget did a classic experiment involving a conservation task to demonstrate this kind of thinking in children. He arranged two sets of coins on a table in two lines. Both sets had the same small number of coins, but the coins in one line were spread farther apart. When asked which line had more coins in it, preoperational children always said the line in which the coins were spread farther apart had more. They held to this belief even when the coins from the two lines were matched up to show that for each coin from the long line, there was a coin from the short line. Conservation tasks, such as this one involving conservation of number, show whether a child has grasped the concept that certain physical characteristics of objects remain the same, even though their outward appearance changes.

Because children at this stage are dependent on their own experience, they tend to make incorrect generalizations. They base their general belief about something on a single experience, which may lead to a false conclusion. One example is the child who believed that a dog's barking makes birds fly. Another is a child in a Virginia child care center whose parents told the teachers that he screamed on the weekend when they attempted to take him for a haircut. "He was hysterical and kept saying it would hurt too much!" the frustrated mother told the teacher. The teacher, who knew a great deal about young children and a little bit about Piaget, slowly explained to the mom that from her son's perspective there was good reason to be afraid of a haircut. By the age of three or four, most youngsters have had enough experience to know that a *cut* on your knee or your finger can hurt quite a bit and sometimes even make you bleed. They know that at preschool, when they make soup, the teachers are very careful to show them how to chop the vegetables so they don't get *cut*. They know that Grandma doesn't let them use her good scissors because they might get *cut*. And then the grown-ups say they're taking you to get your hair *cut?!* The frightened child was overgeneralizing from his limited experience, and when his mother saw the situation from his perspective, his behavior suddenly made more sense to her.

Preoperational children also tend to focus on one attribute of an object or person at a time. It is hard for them to think of their mother as their grandma's daughter, for instance. This single-focus

Chapter 5

thinking is revealed in children's conversations, if adults know how to listen for it. For example, a Head Start teacher tells the story of a little girl in her class whose mom has had a new baby. The teacher shows the children pictures of babies in books. The children discuss how wrinkly and funny-looking babies are when they are born. The teacher tells the children that she heard one boy tell his mother that she should iron the baby. None of the children laugh at this or show any alarm. No one says, "Oh, that is awful. That would hurt the baby."

Instead, Heather says, "My big sister irons her hair to get the curls out."

Joshua says, "That's not what it's for. You do it to get the lines off your clothes."

Clearly, the children do not make the connection that an iron might be a good tool to use on clothes or curly hair but not on babies. These children are not cruel, but they are incapable of holding several qualities of an object or situation in their minds simultaneously. They are focusing on one aspect of the baby (the baby has wrinkles), and one aspect of the iron (the iron is used to get wrinkles out). The children do not naturally consider at the same time that the iron is hot, hot enough to hurt, and that a baby has skin like theirs that could be burned.

The teacher, aware that she has overestimated the children's understanding, can ask questions that make them think a little more about irons. "Is the iron that you use on clothes hot?" she might ask. "How would you feel if you put it next to your skin? Does a baby have skin? How do you think it would feel to the baby's skin?" The children would quickly work out for themselves that an iron is not a good way to get rid of a newborn's wrinkly skin! They know that irons are for getting wrinkles out, but without help, they can't make the distinction between wrinkled clothes and a baby's wrinkled skin. Piaget's theory tells us that it will be more effective to ask questions that help children think through the problem on their own than to tell them flat out, "An iron would hurt the baby." If they construct that knowledge for themselves by puzzling through the teacher's questions, they are more apt to take it in than if the teacher gives it to them.

This characteristic of only seeing one aspect of a thing at a time also plays out in the way children this age take adults very literally (take their words at their exact meaning). For example, Betty cared for Alison, her three-and-a-half-year-old niece, for a weekend. She invited Alison to help her with dinner preparations. At home Alison's mother served her hot dogs on a roll with ketchup already on it. When Betty asked her niece to get the ketchup, Alison asked, "Should I put it on our hot dogs?" Betty, busy in the kitchen, responded, "No, just put it on the table." Betty was surprised when Alison squirted ketchup right onto the dining room table just as she'd been told to do!

Teachers wanting to support the cognitive development of preoperational children in their care can do the following:

- provide large blocks of time for uninterrupted free play
- provide many real-world experiences for children throughout the year
- plan open-ended activities and ask open-ended questions

Provide Large Blocks of Free-Play Time

It is largely the influence of Piaget, building on Montessori's work, that encourages uninterrupted periods of play in early childhood classrooms. When children are interested and involved, they need teachers who respect this absorption with their work. Giving a child a little more time while others clean up for snack can be a way of saying, "I see that you are very involved with your work, and that is important." Sometimes it isn't necessary to completely clean up the room. Children need places where their ongoing work and projects can be left until they are ready to finish them. In times past, children often had abundant opportunities for this kind of ongoing work in their neighborhoods and backyards. It is now our responsibility to meet these needs for sustained projects and "works in progress" in our child care classrooms.

It isn't necessary to pull all the children together for a group time because three or four are having trouble finding an appropriate focus for their energy. Many teachers are finding that snacktime and story time work much better when they are done in several shifts of small groups rather than groups of ten or twelve, with some of the children unable to focus on the task at hand. When children are allowed large blocks of time for sustained interest in their play and work, that usually gives the teachers more time to work one-on-one with those who need it. Organizing some children to do small-group work while others enjoy extended free-play time is how some teachers are making opportunities for more project work for those who are really engaged.

Time outdoors is another gift that teachers can share with children. The natural world provides young children with just as many opportunities to learn and grow across all developmental domains as the indoor classroom does. While it is easy to say that time outdoors should be as rich and meaningful for children as the time spent in the classroom, this is not often the case. Just as teachers need to learn what to do with children indoors to create rich learning experiences for them, they also need to learn what to do with children outdoors. Many teachers are afraid to let children stay outside on a beautiful day because they fear it will be perceived as "doing nothing." A great amount of research has been conducted on the powerful impacts of children being outdoors. The benefits are grand and are not limited to these:

- opportunities to develop gross-motor skills
- time for children to socially interact and use their imaginations

- strengthened emotional development through experiencing various types of emotions, including wonder, joy, surprise, and satisfaction

- stress reduction

When children have regular opportunities to spend time in natural spaces, they learn about the world they live in and come to understand the need to take care of it. Talking with each other and with parents about the importance of taking time in nature to learn is a good place to start.

Many teachers today are frustrated by learning standards that are not developmentally appropriate for the ages of the children they teach but are pushed on them by school districts and state offices. The current age of accountability holds many positive things for teachers and children. For too many years, as discussed in almost every chapter, teachers have misinterpreted progressive education or developmentally appropriate practice as letting the children do whatever suits them. This has resulted in much random wandering and many missed learning opportunities for children. Without careful planning, observation, and documentation, we cannot achieve meaningful curriculum. Accountability that requires observation and documentation can help us strive for excellence. It encourages us to guide all the children to be all that they can be. But problems arise when standards are driven by motives other than what is best for children. Standards requiring all kindergarten children to be reading at a certain level before entering the first grade are both unfair to individual children and unachievable by most teachers.

Reflecting on this aspect of teaching today can help teachers develop strategies for coping with these unrealistic pressures. Teachers, in turn, can help children cope. Talking with each other and with parents about the importance of taking time to learn is a good place to start. Sharing information with parents can help them see that reading and other academic skills should not come at all costs or prior to a certain level of competence at prereading skills.

Provide Real-World Experiences
Like Montessori, Piaget has helped teachers of young children see how important it is for children to experience whatever we want them to learn about. Looking at pictures of cows does not give a child the experience of a cow—its size, smell, sound, and function in our lives. Visiting a dairy farm, smelling the barnyard and the mowed hay, watching machines milk the cows, and seeing the milk loaded into a truck gives children a completely different understanding of cows. Similarly, reading about "things that go" is not a substitute for riding on the subway, in a taxi, or on a train. Providing real-life experiences doesn't have to mean going on field trips. It can be as simple as cooking with children, bringing animals into the classroom, or studying the birds in your area.

It is possible anywhere to find real-life projects for children, even if program resources are stretched thin. In rural New Hampshire, a team of Head Start teachers on a limited budget did a project with children on building. They visited a lumbering site and watched trees being cut and processed. They went to a construction area where a neighbor was having a house built, and then they realized they knew little about the building their school occupied. The custodian got involved. Children viewed the plumbing and electrical systems in the school. They did tracings of brick surfaces, floors, and other areas. The play that went on in woodworking and blocks showed a much deeper understanding of many construction principles than one usually views in a preschool room. This is what construction of knowledge is all about for young children.

Plan Open-Ended Activities, Ask Open-Ended Questions
Open-ended activities do not have a predetermined result or product. For example, when a teacher plans a science activity with a known

outcome, it is not an open-ended experiment. However, when children plant seeds and chart the days until the shoots break through the earth, and then measure the seedlings every day and keep graphs of how they grow, the project is open-ended. Neither the adult nor the children know what the result will be.

Similarly, open-ended questions do not have predetermined answers. "What color is your shirt?" is a closed question: There is probably only one right answer, and the teacher knows what it is. "How do you think that works?" is an open-ended question: The teacher is asking children for their reasoning and doesn't already know the answer.

Open-ended activities and questions support children's cognitive development because they ask children to think. Instead of putting children in the position of being right or wrong, they put them in the position of inquiry, of finding out what the possibilities are, or observing how fast the bean sprout grows. They help children look at several aspects of the same thing, as the teacher's questions about the hot iron and the baby's skin helped those children think about the consequences of ironing a baby. They help children accommodate new information. For example, take the child who thinks that a dog's barking makes the birds fly. Over time, an adult who knew that the child had formed this idea about the world could help them adjust it by noticing dogs barking and birds flying and asking careful open-ended questions, such as "I heard that dog bark behind the house, and look, those birds are sitting on the fence. Why do you suppose that is?" or "Look, there's a group of ducks taking off from the pond. Did you hear any dogs barking? Why do you suppose those ducks took flight?"

The Concrete Operations and Formal Operations Stages

The last two stages in Piaget's theory refer to school-age children and teenagers. Since the focus of this book is on the early childhood years, the discussion of these stages will be brief. It is helpful to all parents and teachers to know a little bit about these final stages. For more information, see the suggested reading list at the end of the chapter.

When children enter Piaget's stage of concrete operations at about age seven, many changes in their thought patterns are visible. At this age (usually from about age seven through eleven or twelve) children possess the characteristic of reversibility, which allows them to reverse the direction of their thought. For example, children at this stage can retrace their steps on the schoolyard looking for a forgotten lunch box. Children no longer count on their fingers, because they are beginning to be able to think abstractly. They begin to notice differences in classes of objects. For instance, at age four, every dog is a "doggie," but at age eight or nine, children see differences between a collie and a poodle. The concrete-operational child can hold several qualities in mind, knowing that a boat is large, red, *and* a sailboat. They know and really understand that their mother is also the daughter of their grandmother. With this new flexibility of thought, children can add, subtract, and multiply in their heads.

The final stage Piaget outlined is formal operations. This stage begins between ages eleven and sixteen and is marked by the ability to think logically and in hypothetical terms. According to Piaget, once this stage is reached, young people can wrestle with such questions as "Is it wrong to steal food for your starving children?" or "If a tree falls in the forest and no one is there to hear it, does it make a sound?"

Piaget in the Twenty-First Century

The quote from Elizabeth Jones earlier in this chapter is still so relevant to approaching theory over time. The foundational theorists of our field gave us such direction in understanding the developmental needs of young children that they are not diminished or discredited by changes in society or knowledge that force us to make adaptations to their original work. Much has been made in recent years of the fact that we now see a capacity for empathy in young children that Piaget implied was not consistent with their developmental egocentrism. I like to think of this fact as a positive indication that more young children are getting their attachment needs met in infancy. Erikson asserted that meeting those needs consistently in infancy would result in a greater capacity for empathy.

Discussion Questions

1. Quinn, one of the nine-month-old babies in your infant program has always transitioned easily in the morning. You can tell from several clues that she has recently achieved object permanence. She begins to fuss and cry at separation from her parents in the morning, and they are alarmed at the behavior, believing she is no longer happy in your program. You are convinced that her recent clinginess is related to her development. How can you explain this to her parents?

2. Kevin is a four-year-old in your preschool class. He is very interested in building. He wants to spend all his time in the block area. Kevin's mom worries that he plays too much. She has asked you to teach him math and language skills. Drawing on Piaget's work, how can you respond in a supportive way to this parent?

3. On a trip to the children's museum with your class of three-year-olds, a parent volunteer approaches you with one of the children in hand and says, "I just caught this one shoplifting!" How do you handle this situation? What do you say to the parent? What do you say to the child? How do you talk to the museum staff? How can Piaget's theories help explain what has happened?

Chapter 5

Suggestions for Further Reading

Forman, George E., and David S. Kuschner. 1983. *The Child's Construction of Knowledge: Piaget for Teaching Children*. National Association for the Education of Young Children.

Furth, Hans G., and Harry Wachs. 1975. *Thinking Goes to School: Piaget's Theory in Practice*. Oxford University Press.

Singer, Dorothy G., and Tracey A. Revenson. 1996. *A Piaget Primer: How a Child Thinks*. Revised ed. Plume.

Chapter 6: John Bowlby

When a baby is born he cannot tell one person from another and indeed can hardly tell person from thing. Yet, by his first birthday he is likely to have become a connoisseur of people. Not only does he come quickly to distinguish familiars from strangers but amongst his familiars he chooses one or more favorites. They are greeted with delight; they are followed when they depart; and they are sought when absent. Their loss causes anxiety and distress; their recovery, relief and a sense of security. On this foundation, it seems, the rest of his emotional life is built—without this foundation there is risk for his future happiness and health.

—**John Bowlby, foreword to** *Infancy in Uganda: Infant care and the growth of love*, **by Mary Ainsworth**

Biography

JOHN BOWLBY WAS BORN in London in 1907. He was the fourth of six children in a traditional, upper-middle-class English family. As was the fashion for his class and time, Bowlby and his siblings were raised by nannies and had very little contact with their parents. Middle-class women at the time believed parental attention and affection resulted in lack of discipline. The children typically spent an hour a day at teatime with their mother. Bowlby had one nanny to whom he was quite attached. She left the family's employ when he was four years old. As an adult, Bowlby described this loss as similar to the loss of a mother. At seven, again typically for his social class, he was sent to boarding school. He remembered this as a terrible

Chapter 6

time in his life. Bowlby's lifework focused on the effects of early separation and loss on lifespan development. It has been said that his own childhood experiences drove his professional interest and gave him tremendous sensitivity to the suffering of young children.

Bowlby's father was a surgeon. He directed John to medical school. Bowlby was an excellent student and won prizes for outstanding intellectual achievement. He began his career at Trinity College, Cambridge. He took time after college to volunteer for children with serious emotional and behavioral challenges. From the beginning, Bowlby was interested in the connections between family life and children's mental health and behavior. Though this is a common field of study in child growth and development today, it was uncommon at the time.

A friend urged Bowlby to change the direction of his study from medicine to psychology. While still in medical school, he enrolled in the Institute for Psychoanalysis. Though qualified in both medicine and psychoanalysis, Bowlby's sustained interest was in the mental and emotional health of children. From his earliest studies, Bowlby was convinced that deviant or troubled behaviors in late childhood and adolescence had their origins in the family system. He believed the first relationships in infancy set the tone for all later love relationships. He believed that disruption to these first relationships or poor quality in these relationships accounted for trauma and troubling behaviors in adolescence and adult life.

His ideas were not well received in the psychoanalytic community. It was the prevailing thought at the time that one needed to look inside the mind at dreams and fantasies to determine the source of neuroses or deviant behaviors. The analysis of troubled individuals was the foundation of psychoanalytic studies. Bowlby believed that observation would yield more information about an individual's reality. He believed the troubled youth he worked with experienced problems because of external causes rooted in their homes and in the earliest experiences that had occurred there—or in the situations that ideally should have occurred there but did not.

Bowlby's Theories

Bowlby's first professional papers present the idea that two environmental factors early in life can present lifetime challenges for individuals. The first of these, which received much negative attention in his early career, is that separation from or death of a mother results in lifelong struggles for the individual. The second, which today seems like an ordinary idea, is that the emotional attitude of a parent toward a child has life-shaping effects.

Bowlby proposes that often the attitude of a parent toward a child is deeply affected by unresolved issues from his or her own childhood. Today these ideas are widely accepted by psychologists, educators, and sociologists and are part of the well-known foundations of development. When Bowlby first presented his ideas, they were not taken seriously by academicians in any discipline.

At the time, analysts tended to focus on problems around feeding, toileting, or exposure to parents' sexual intercourse. All of these issues and their interpretations tended to flow from Freud's theory and practice of psychoanalysis. So when Bowlby suggested that observations of parental behaviors in the home might provide a clue to a child's development, he was largely dismissed by the psychoanalytic community. Bowlby's work revolved around observation and human experience and interaction. This type of research was new, and at the time, analysts did not consider it their job to give any consideration at all to the real experiences of patients.

Bowlby was single-minded in his work. The fact that few found his work as fascinating as he did was not discouraging to him. He was certain he had discovered a key to unlocking the mysteries of deviant human behavior and distress. He spent his life trying to understand the effects of early relationships on mental health and stability in adulthood. It has often been said of Bowlby that he was shy and distant and that these characteristics, as well as his interest in early childhood, were based on his own unhappy childhood. Bowlby had tremendous insight into the lives of children. In his later years, he spoke passionately about the ways that society should respond to the needs of young children. His criticism of patterns of child rearing that were isolating or harsh could be viewed as his indictment of his own childhood.

Throughout his career, Bowlby struggled with the fact that his fellow psychoanalysts did not acknowledge his findings. He was unable to provide a scientific explanation for what he knew to be true from his observations of children and families. His goals for establishing a more sensitive model of developmental psychology were challenged by the psychoanalytic community while he was researching attachment and loss. Bowlby felt certain his understanding was key to a more progressive model, but at the time, nearly all research was quantitative (using numerical data to measure and test). Today qualitative research studies (exploring experience, based on nonnumerical data such as observations or interviews) are met with respect that did not exist in Bowlby's time. The dilemma was in establishing numerical values for such qualities as abusiveness, unkindness, and mistreatment, even when these were acknowledged by the psychoanalytic community. Bowlby was sure that beyond actual abuse or cruelty, unresponsive or manipulative parenting styles contributed to later mental health problems in individuals.

It was for these reasons that Bowlby is best known for his studies on and theories of attachment based on early parent-child separation. It was not that attachment theory captured his interest more than other broad areas of early development, but parent-child separation could be easily documented and was less open to interpretation or misunderstanding than, for example, determining what might constitute unresponsive maternal behavior.

His interests were far-reaching and ahead of his time. Bowlby advocated early intervention and worked tirelessly to change national policies in support of young children and their families. For example, the Perry Preschool Project of the 1960s captured the interest of contemporary politicians and the media for its emphasis on addressing the problems of the youngest citizens before they needed remedial services or juvenile interventions because of crimes committed.

Bowlby's work with troubled youths led him to believe that the following are critical questions to be asked:

- What conditions in a child's rearing lead to stability and strength rather than deviance?

- How can we nurture such strengths?

- How can we help young children see that everyone has positive and negative thoughts and feelings about the people they love?

- How do we give serious attention to the costs of early separation from family?

- What policies can be put in place to avert these separations?

Bowlby fought to send the message that policies needed changing. For example, he believed that families, especially economically disadvantaged ones, needed greater assistance. He thought that more people should be trained professionally in marriage and child guidance and in working with parents of the very young. He wanted the public to understand that the funds required to put supportive programs in place would be far less than the later costs of institutional care and delinquency (Bowlby 1951).

Some critics, such as Marga Vicedo (2017), have taken Bowlby and his theories to task, arguing the emphasis on mothers as preferred caregivers is inherently sexist. At the same time, Bowlby has often been accused of being too hard on mothers, but much of this impression has come from words taken out of context or popularized by his opponents. He was actually a man of great empathy for motherhood. He knew mothering was the hardest and least appreciated job, and he often criticized government and social agencies for not being more appreciative or proactive in supporting young parents. As Brian Allen (2023, 35), author of *The Science and Clinical Practice of Attachment Theory*, explains, "Bowlby's goal was to make the public mindful of the importance of real-life parent–child relationships on child development, not to confront gender bias."

Chapter 6

Bowlby observed that comments about parenthood were often made glibly by those who had not experienced it and that people should be more cautious with their indictments. He was sympathetic to the plight of ordinary children raised in an era in which adults gave little attention to the pressing needs and fears of children. He was a proponent of progressive education and believed that children needed attention, affection, and freedom to develop optimally (Bowlby 1940). None of these interests have become as prominent a part of Bowlby's legacy as his work on maternal deprivation.

Post–World War II England provided optimal conditions for Bowlby's work. Institutions were full of infants abandoned or orphaned during the war. In addition to the film René Spitz was making on institutionalized infants, Harry Harlow's work at the University of Wisconsin gave the scientific community reason to reevaluate its position on nourishment as the basis for an infant's attachment to the mother. In Harlow's studies, rhesus monkeys were deprived of their mothers and then given either a terry cloth mother to provide "contact comfort" (Allen 2023, 42) or a wire one that provided food. Harlow's studies dealt the first scientific blow to the belief that affectional ties were based on nursing: For rhesus monkeys, at least, cuddly contact proved far more important to attachment and survival—a fact that brought great joy to the Bowlby camp (Harlow 1958). The fact that monkeys exposed to terry cloth mothers survived at a higher rate than those whose wire mothers offered nourishment but no comfort was a huge step forward to those engaged in attachment studies. (Later studies with the rhesus monkeys indicated that the early separation from biological parents left these monkeys vulnerable to poor peer relationships and diminished ability to raise their young.) There was no doubt that Harlow's studies confirmed the work of Bowlby and others who stated the case for relationships as significant to emotional health. Harlow proved that comfort is a need of the very young as well as a factor in infant feeding. Bowlby was grateful for Harlow's contributions to the discussion of attachment behaviors.

Harlow modeled his research on Bowlby's previous observations with children and found similar indications of protest and detachment with his monkeys (Suomi et al., 2008).

Bowlby in the Twenty-First Century

Current understanding of growth and development and psychology force us to acknowledge that Bowlby's work overstates the necessity of mother-child attachment. Most contemporary theorists assume that what does and doesn't happen during the earliest stages of life affect development for a lifetime in powerful ways. Unmet needs in infancy continue to haunt us until they are eventually reconciled. This assumption is called infant determinism. Jean Mercer points out that we rarely question this premise, even though the evidence to support it is not conclusive. She suggests that not enough research has been done to identify the ways in which later social experiences and relationships also affect adult development (Mercer 2006). The work of Erik Erikson encouraged developmental theorists to believe that significant needs for love and trust continue to be present in life's challenges. Erikson (1968) proposes that opportunities to resolve these unmet needs surface again and again until one is able to adequately meet one's needs for love and trust.

Harvard's Jerome Kagan (1998, 94) goes so far as to identify infant determinism as a "seductive idea" that should be approached with caution. Each historical era and its attending sociological conditions shape any body of research as well as the public's reaction to it. According to Kagan, "The swell of enthusiasm for attachment theory was also, in part, an understandable reaction to the excessive cruelties of the Second World War. The atrocities generated a desire among psychologists and psychiatrists for a conception of human nature with less dark, Freudian pessimism. Erik Erikson's creative intuition to replace Freud's oral stage with a stage of trust satisfied this hunger for a more humane, less selfish infant who was receptive to parental love."

Kagan (1998, 95) believes that Bowlby "sensed that the angst of his historical era was a rupture of family and social bonds, and he guessed that a child's secure attachment to a parent protected her from fear and inoculated her against future uneasiness." In previous centuries, Kagan writes, "parents wanted their children to be able to cope with adversity, but they thought forcing their children to cope with difficulty was a better preparation for life than showering them with love and protecting them from worry."

It is important in concluding discussion of Bowlby's theory of attachment to note that scientific study of human development includes looking at how things change and how they remain the same. There is no doubt that Bowlby, the father of attachment theory, contributed enormously to our understanding of the human condition. It is important for us to take his theories and test them against contemporary observations in early childhood development and education. We must also acknowledge his work as a foundation for all of us who study children and families and who view emotional connections as critical to healthy human development and success in adult life.

Discussion Questions

1. How does Bowlby's theory inform child care policies to prioritize relationship-based care in early childhood settings?

2. In what ways can understanding attachment theory help child care professionals better support children's social and emotional development throughout their lives?

3. How can child care practices help minimize the negative effects of separation anxiety and build trust during transitions, such as arriving at the program or switching caregivers?

Suggestions for Further Reading

Bowlby, John. 1951. *Maternal Care and Mental Health*. World Health Organization.

———. 1970. *Child Care and the Growth of Love*. 2nd ed. Pelican.

———. 1982, 1980, 1973. *Attachment and Loss*. Vols. 1, 2, and 3. Basic Books.

Holmes, Jeremy. 2014. *John Bowlby and Attachment Theory*. 2nd ed. Routledge.

Stern, Jessica A., Stephanie Irby Coard, Oscar A. Barbarin, and Jude Cassidy. 2024. "What Attachment Scholars Can Learn from Research on Black Family Resilience." *Child Development Perspectives* 18:10–18.

Cliffe, Johanna, and Carla Solvason. 2023. "What Is It That We Still Don't Get? Relational Pedagogy and Why Relationships and Connections Matter in Early Childhood." *Power and Education* 15, no. 3 (November): 259–73.

Chapter 7: Mary Ainsworth

I did not intend this as a way of assessing attachment, but it certainly wound up as that. We began to realize that it fit in with our impressions after seventy-two hours of observation in an amazing way. But instead of seventy-two hours of observation we could do a Strange Situation in twenty minutes.

—**Mary Ainsworth**, *Becoming Attached*

Biography

MARY AINSWORTH'S DESCRIPTION OF HER now-famous Strange Situation gives us a peek at the no-nonsense woman who created it. Mary Dinsmore Salter was born in Glendale, Ohio, in 1913. She was the oldest of three daughters. Her parents were college educated and provided a middle-class life for their family. The Salter girls enjoyed a comfortable home life and many rich educational opportunities. The family moved to Canada when Mary was five years old. Her education, from a bachelor's degree through her doctorate, was completed at the University of Toronto.

Though Ainsworth's childhood has been described as ideal, there were troubling emotional currents in the home that led her to feel her childhood had somehow failed her. Her own insecurities led her to passionately pursue a career that questioned how secure attachment was formed. She studied theories on security as the primary foundation of a healthy personality. When she took an abnormal-psychology course, she looked at the close relationship between parents and children as a cornerstone to secure feelings for young

Chapter 7

children. She shared thoughts on these pieces of her own development in a series of interviews with Robert Karen (1998) that are included in his book *Becoming Attached*.

In 1950 Mary Salter married Leonard Ainsworth. She moved with him to London, where he finished his graduate work and she answered an advertisement in the *London Times* for a research assistant. The ad had been placed by John Bowlby. Answering that ad proved to have an enormous impact on the direction her lifework would take, as it did on John Bowlby's work.

Bowlby recognized at once that Ainsworth had a brilliant mind and a passion for research. He was excited that her education, interests, and early research were much like his own. Like Bowlby, Ainsworth (1967) was convinced that observation of infants in their home environment was a more accurate way to assess emotional stability and attachments than focusing on the memories and dreams of insecure adults. Thus, like Bowlby, her approach was contrary to common practice of the psychoanalytic community. In their initial interview, Bowlby saw that Ainsworth was an independent thinker who was experienced and intelligent enough to know what could be validated by empirical data and what could not. Both researchers struggled throughout their careers with the significance of empirical data. They trusted their gut responses and knew their observations in natural settings provided information as important as what could be quantified in a laboratory setting.

Like Bowlby, Ainsworth believed her research, and psychology in general, could be used to improve the human condition. So she moved forward with enthusiasm and conviction, even when others in the academic community judged her harshly. She worked with Bowlby for three and a half years, and their collaboration fed each other's work for the rest of their lives. This mutual interest and support was very much in evidence in 1961, when Bowlby asked Ainsworth to represent him at the World Health Organization. Karen (1998, 123) describes Ainsworth's efforts on Bowlby's behalf:

Ainsworth produced a brilliantly coherent statement of Bowlby's and her views. For the first time in one place she clarified many of the misunderstandings, successfully repudiated oft-repeated criticisms, and smoothed out some of Bowlby's own apparent inconsistencies and dubious hunches. Ainsworth broke the debate down into its constituent parts. She noted that the catch-all phrase "maternal deprivation" was actually composed of three different dimensions—the lack of maternal care (insufficiency), distortion of maternal care (neglect or mistreatment), and discontinuity in maternal care (separations, or the child's being given one mother figure and then another)—and that these three dimensions were frequently confounded, making it difficult to study any one of them alone. Carefully sifting through dozens of studies, she assessed what they had to say about the effects of each of these conditions, and, in doing so, she was able to disentangle many apparent contradictions.

Bowlby had refined his work to focus on discontinuity of care. Like Ainsworth, he was interested in maternal deprivation but found it easier to apply scientific method to one aspect of maternal deprivation than to the other two dimensions Ainsworth had so clearly outlined for the World Health Organization. Ainsworth moved beyond maternal deprivation to study other aspects of infant development. She knew even as a student that she would one day focus on the relationships of infants and mothers during the first year of life.

Ainsworth's Research and Theories

In 1954, Mary Ainsworth followed her husband from London to Uganda, where he had accepted a teaching position. She secured a small grant from the East African Institute of Social Research and spent a month with other researchers, learning the language and customs of the Ugandan people. With few resources but great enthusiasm, she began one of the earliest studies on infant development in the twentieth century.

When Ainsworth began her research, she still believed that attachment behavior in human infants was associated with the experience of feeding. But Ainsworth was an expert at observation. As she watched infants and mothers in their own home environments, she began to see the picture as much broader and deeper than theorists suggested. Her style was different from the laboratory research then being done in Europe and the United States. She approached the women in Uganda as an outsider who was interested in learning from and about them. She also presented herself as a friend and helper. She and her associates went into women's homes at regular intervals and did whatever needed to be done to support and help these parents. She got to know them. She got to know their infants. She began developing lists of behaviors that she believed were an indication of an attachment between mothers and their babies.

As her lists developed, they included behaviors like these (Ainsworth 1967):

- crying when mother leaves
- following mother
- showing concern for mother's whereabouts
- scrambling over mother
- burying face in mother's lap
- using mother as a safe haven when in a strange situation
- flying to mother when frightened
- greeting mother through smiling, crowing, clapping, lifting arms, and general excitement

Ainsworth noticed that once babies were able to crawl and walk, they moved away from their mothers to explore their surroundings. If a surprising or different element entered their surroundings, these babies immediately headed back to their mothers. She observed this behavior in so many of the infants that it led her to hypothesize that babies use their mothers as a secure base to depart from and return to in their explorations of the world. Returning to her initial studies of security, she suggested that securely attached infants had the courage to leave their mothers and investigate their surroundings, knowing they could return to their mothers if they became anxious.

It also occurred to Ainsworth that a broad range of differences in development and style existed among babies and mothers as they worked on the development of relationships. She decided that a very complex set of circumstances contributed to the mother-child relationship. She saw many differences in development from child to child. She concluded that methods of care varied from culture to culture and affected these relationships as well. She noted that many anxious babies seemed to be the offspring of anxious mothers. She noticed that mothers separated from their husbands or families experienced more stress and seemed to pass it on to their infants (Ainsworth 1967).

Ainsworth found it difficult to articulate clear lists of variables indicating secure and insecure attachment. She understood the complexity of her subject matter. She knew that determining precise variables is not easy when observing infants and mothers; multiple causes affect the outcomes.

Ainsworth found that mothers who give the most care to their young have infants who are securely attached, while mothers who are not present for their infants have babies who are less securely attached. She was quick to realize that there are exceptions to these observations. Are quantity and quality of care then equivalent? Ainsworth thought not. She believed the quality of the care must be an important factor, but she could not prove this. As a fastidious researcher, Ainsworth struggled to make sense of all the information she had collected. Her book *Infancy in Uganda* was not published until 1967, long after her studies in Uganda were behind her.

In 1956 Mary Ainsworth once again moved to accompany her husband, this time to a new job in the United States. Mary soon found a position at Johns Hopkins University in Baltimore. She taught courses on personality assessment but longed to replicate her study of infants and mothers in the United States. It was many years before she was able to convince Johns Hopkins to fund her work. In 1963 she was awarded a grant, which was meager, but her interest in and passion for research were keen. Like her work in Uganda, Ainsworth's Baltimore research was conducted in what was still considered an unusual fashion. She and her colleagues did their observations in home settings and took detailed notes to assess a child's response to everyday separations. Although Ainsworth hoped to pick up her earlier study, in the years since she had conducted it, several other questions had surfaced. Ainsworth now wondered, for example, if attachment behaviors were universal. Would she see a different array of behaviors in the United States? Today studying behavior in the context of culture is commonplace. In the early 1960s in Baltimore, Maryland, Mary Ainsworth was a pioneer of cultural research.

When Ainsworth compared the data from her Baltimore study to that from her Uganda study, she was delighted to observe "similarities relating to the structure and function of infant attachment behavior across the two contexts" (Allen 2023, 53). She believed that babies studied around the world would demonstrate similar behaviors when separated from their mothers. She wanted to pursue her idea of the mother as a secure base. Ainsworth argued that although home observations were important for observing infant behavior in accordance with their caregiver, a problem arose. Infants often were interested in the staff coming into the home and did not display behavior where children needed to be close to their family members, which Bowlby would describe as attachment behavior. She decided that if she and her colleagues could not test for the "secure base" in Baltimore homes, they would set up a "strange situation" on the university campus. There they could observe the babies reacting to their mother's departures in a more stressful environment.

Ainsworth and her colleagues knew what they wanted to observe. They decided on a room filled with engaging toys. They would observe a baby as they explored this new space with their mother nearby. Researchers would then introduce a stranger to the room to increase the stress level. They would check the infant's response. They would then have the mother leave the baby alone in the room with the stranger. They would observe the infant's behavior at separation and at reunion.

The procedure was called the Strange Situation, and it has become a widely used, well-validated method of determining an infant's attachment behaviors to her caregivers. It is by far the most well-known piece of Ainsworth's work. The Strange Situation is included in most texts on infant development. It is briefly described as a twenty-minute observation of infant play in an unfamiliar room while both familiar and unfamiliar adults enter and leave the room. Its purpose is to determine a child's attachment behaviors based on the usual comings and goings of significant adults as well as on documented responses to unfamiliar adults. The child's responses are observed and documented as the child experiences this sequence of events:

1. Parent and infant are introduced to the experimental room.

2. Parent and infant are alone. Parent does not participate while infant explores.

3. Stranger enters, converses with parent, then approaches infant. Parent leaves inconspicuously.

4. First separation episode: Stranger's behavior is geared to that of infant.

5. First reunion episode: Parent greets and comforts infant, then leaves again.

6. Second separation episode: Infant is alone.

7. Continuation of second separation episode: Stranger enters and gears behavior to that of infant.

8. Second reunion episode: Parent enters, greets infant, and picks up infant. Stranger leaves inconspicuously.

Throughout this process, researchers observe two aspects of the child's behavior:

- the amount of exploration the child engages in throughout the process
- the child's reactions to the departure and return of the parent or primary caregiver

Results of the Strange Situation categorize infant behaviors into three forms of attachment behavior:

- secure attachment
- anxious-ambivalent insecure attachment
- anxious-avoidant insecure attachment

The child described as securely attached to an adult explores their surroundings with enthusiasm, checking back with their secure base (mother, father, or primary caregiver) periodically. During the Strange Situation, the securely attached infant engages with strangers if their mother is nearby, cries when their mother leaves the room, is happy to reunite with their mother when she returns, and does not engage with strangers if their mother is not nearby. The securely attached child tends to develop a sense of security that allows them to cope with problems and to adapt well to unfamiliar situations. Parents of securely attached infants tend to be responsive and sensitive to their infant's needs in an appropriate way. This style of attachment behavior is marked by both the positive, close relationship with the parent or caregiver and the infant's willingness to be independent in exploring their surroundings. This is the child who typifies the "secure base" theory. They snuggle happily with their caregiver, then wiggle down to check out the space and the toys or just to wander. They look back to check that their caregiver is still present or simply to smile. They return now and again for encouragement or if a situation makes them feel uncomfortable. The securely attached child is both comfortable and confident.

The child assessed as anxious-ambivalent insecurely attached tends to express distress when near strangers or in unfamiliar settings, regardless of whether the parent or caregiver is nearby. The child exhibits extreme anxiety and distress when the parent departs and yet is often resistant to reuniting when the parent returns. This style of attachment is confusing to researchers, parents, and providers. Some psychologists suggest that the style is the result of inconsistent parenting. Ainsworth suggests that the parent responds to the child on the parent's own schedule rather than the infant's. It is difficult for both parents and infants when anxious-ambivalent attachment patterns set in.

The anxious-avoidant insecurely attached assessment is perhaps the most challenging of all attachment behaviors to understand and support. These infants show little behavior indicating interest in the adults in the room, regardless of which adults are present. They tend to avoid or ignore both parents and primary caregivers, whether strangers are nearby or not. These children treat strangers similarly to how they treat parents or primary providers. They show little emotional response. Some of these babies react exactly the same way when they are in the room with parents, primary caregivers, strangers, or no one. Infants assessed with anxious-avoidant insecure attachment react in a style to that of the orphaned and abandoned infants studied by Bowlby and Spitz. They lack affect. These babies don't seem to believe they can influence their fate. They don't seem to believe that adults in their lives will respond to their signals of distress. These children come to believe that communication of their needs makes no difference at all.

In reviewing the three attachment styles outlined by Ainsworth and her colleagues, we can't help but ask certain questions. For instance, if a parent is emotionally unavailable to an infant's signals because of unemployment, substance abuse, or other real issues in the lives of young families, what happens if those circumstances change? As practitioners, we need to remind parents and each other that circumstances for children and parents are constantly changing. For example, a child who is insecurely attached at age one may become securely attached by age two, and this would considerably brighten ideas about any long-term effects of insecure attachment. The idea that early relationships do not necessarily determine later social relationships is important. When we are more flexible in our views about attachment as a changing characteristic, we provide a stronger basis for intervention and family support.

Ainsworth in the Twenty-First Century

As we think about attachment behaviors and their ability to change over time, we can thank Mary Ainsworth for first calling our attention to this important part of human growth and development. Her contributions took Bowlby's initial work on infants and innovated by creating a method of classifying the behavior observed. Because she was rigorous in her pursuit of valid research, she not only contributed to our body of foundational infant research but also paved the way for others after her to emphasize the importance of direct observation. She earned the respect of her colleagues for her careful, direct observations while proving that observations of infants and mothers in their home environments could lead us to important research questions that might never have surfaced otherwise.

Ainsworth died in Charlottesville, Virginia, at the age of eighty-five, retired from the University of Virginia, but she had continued to be active in her work until the very end of her life. Kurt Vonnegut (1999, 21) referred to her obituary in *The New York Times* as "extravagantly favorable." It stated that Mary Ainsworth had contributed more to our knowledge of infant-parent attachment than anyone else who had researched it. It noted that her reference to absent-minded lack of bonding was also a significant contribution to the field. Many students of growth and development are in tune with dramatic losses and interruptions that affect attachment. Ainsworth called our attention to the routine ways that this relationship can be compromised if we are not mindful of its importance. Her research in London, Uganda, and the United States encouraged discussion about the need of infants for secure attachments. Although her belief that an individual will remain anxious if this first relationship goes awry is still hotly debated, without Ainsworth's input, the conversation would not be part of our continued search for the keys to emotional stability and comfort.

Discussion Questions

1. As educators, we need to remember that circumstances for families are constantly changing. Consider a family whose child is enrolled in your child care setting. What might you want to learn from and about this family to better understand their child's needs? How can we support children and families and demonstrate flexibility in response to life outside of a child care program?

2. How does Ainsworth's emphasis on a "secure base" translate to the physical and emotional environment within our child care setting?

Chapter 7

Suggestions for Further Readings

Ainsworth, Mary D. Salter. 1967. *Infancy in Uganda: Infant Care and the Growth of Love.* Johns Hopkins Press.

Allen, Brian. 2023. *The Science and Clinical Practice of Attachment Theory: A Guide from Infancy to Adulthood.* American Psychological Association.

Mercer, Jean. 2006. *Understanding Attachment: Parenting, Child Care, and Emotional Development.* Praeger Publishers.

Saltman, Bethany. 2021. *Strange Situation: A Mother's Journey into the Science of Attachment.* Ballantine Books.

Viorst, Judith. 1998. *Necessary Losses: The Loves, Illusions, Dependencies, and Impossible Expectations That All of Us Have to Give Up in Order to Grow.* Simon & Schuster.

Chapter 8: Lev Vygotsky

Learning and development are interrelated from the child's very first day of life.

—**Lev Vygotsky,** *Mind in Society*

Biography

Lev Vygotsky was born in Russia in 1896. His family was part of Russia's middle class. They encouraged his studies. Vygotsky graduated from the University of Moscow in 1917 with a specialization in literature. He then taught literature in secondary school. This experience intensified his interest in teaching and in how people learn. He was particularly interested in cognitive and language development and their relationships to learning. This led to his interest in psychology and its impact on educational theory. Vygotsky studied and responded to the work of contemporaries Sigmund Freud, Jean Piaget, and Maria Montessori. He searched for answers to the questions raised by his interest in children and their approach to learning new things. That search involved his discovery that in a group of children at the same developmental level, some children were able to learn with a little help while other children were not. This piece of Vygotsky's learning is a cornerstone for the theories he developed.

It is hard to say what impact Vygotsky's perspective could have brought to our field with the passage of time. His brilliant career was cut short when he died of tuberculosis in 1934 at the age of thirty-eight. Many believe that his impact on educators in the United States was overshadowed by the huge popularity of Piaget's theories, which were enthusiastically embraced in US preschools in the 1960s and continue to guide many classroom practices today.

In recent years, many early childhood educators in the United States have turned their attention to the preschools in Reggio Emilia, Italy. Discussion of the educational theories implemented there has brought about a new focus on Vygotsky's work. Vygotsky's sociocultural perspective, for example, provides a theoretical basis for a Reggio-inspired approach to early childhood education.

Vygotsky's Theories

Vygotsky's ideas were and continue to be controversial. Because he came to the field without specific training in psychology and development, he brought a fresh perspective to child study. He objected to the analysis of children's abilities based on intelligence tests. He thought research should be both qualitative and quantitative. By this he meant that careful observation (qualitative research) of children should be considered as valid as their scores on a test (quantitative research).

Vygotsky has changed the way educators think about children's interactions with others. His work showed that social and cognitive development work together and build on each other. For years early educators, schooled in Piaget's theories, viewed children's knowledge as being constructed from personal experiences. Although Vygotsky also believed this, he thought that personal and social experience cannot be separated. The world children inhabit is shaped by their families, communities, socioeconomic status, education, and culture. Their understanding of this world comes partly from the values and beliefs of the adults and other children in their lives. Children learn from each other every day. They develop language skills and grasp new concepts as they speak to and listen to each other.

Like Piaget, Vygotsky believed that much learning takes place when children play. He believed that language and development build on each other. When children play, they constantly use language. They determine the conditions of the make-believe. They discuss roles and objects and directions. They correct each other. They learn about situations and ideas not yet tried. Vygotsky believed that this interaction contributes to children's construction of knowledge—to their learning. Vygotsky's primary contribution to our understanding of young children's development is the importance of interaction with teachers and peers in advancing children's knowledge. Today's Reggio-inspired educators also believe that what children learn from their peers and the materials in the classroom are as important as what they learn from their teachers.

The Zone of Proximal Development

One of the most important concepts of Vygotsky's theory is that of the zone of proximal development (ZPD). Vygotsky defined this as the distance between the most difficult task a child can do alone and the most difficult task a child can do with help. He believed that a child on the verge of learning a new concept can benefit from interaction with a teacher or a classmate.

Vygotsky referred to the assistance a teacher or peer offers a child as scaffolding. A housepainter working on a house uses a scaffold to reach parts of the house that would otherwise be out of reach. In the same way, adults and peers can help a child "reach" a new concept or skill by giving supporting information. Vygotsky believed this could be done not only by the teacher but also by the child's peers who already possess the desired skill. Vygotsky believed that to scaffold well for children, teachers need to be keen observers. He believed that teachers need to use their observations to determine where children are in a learning process and where they are capable of going, given their individual needs and the social context that surrounds them. He believed that from information gathered through observation, teachers can support children's learning. This is similar to Dewey's belief that teachers must use their greater knowledge of the world to help make sense of it for children.

Teachers who want to apply Vygotsky's ideas about ZPD and scaffolding in their early childhood programs can observe children carefully and plan curriculum that encourages children's emerging abilities and stretches their competence, and pair up children who can learn from each other.

Observe Children Closely and Plan Curriculum Accordingly
Like Montessori and Piaget, Vygotsky emphasized the importance of observation. By carefully watching and listening, teachers come to know each child's development. According to Vygotsky, this is the only way for teachers to accurately assess what is within a child's ZPD at any time. This knowledge is essential to good curriculum planning.

Curriculum planning is perhaps the area most affected by Vygotsky's theory. Unlike Piaget, who thought children's cognitive learning is more internal than interactive, Vygotsky believed that interaction has a huge impact on cognitive development. Until Vygotsky's work became better known in the United States, US educators who understood Piaget's theory hesitated to "push" children. Piaget believed that stages of cognitive development are tied to physical development. He thought that children at a particular stage of development are incapable of the reasoning that they will grow into at the next stage. This led teachers to plan curriculum that supported children at their current level of expected development without stretching their developmental limits.

Vygotsky, on the other hand, showed that children's cognitive development is affected not only by their physical development but also by their social surroundings and interactions. His idea of developmental readiness is more flexible than Piaget's because it encompasses the skills or ideas that children have not yet come to on their own but that they can acquire from the example of peers or adults. This theory encourages teachers to plan curriculum that extends children's knowledge and to scaffold their learning by putting them in situations where their competence is stretched.

Plan Challenging Curriculum to Stretch Children's Competence

Here's an example of a teacher focusing on the ZPD of one of her students, a girl named Margaret. It also illustrates how both the teacher and the child's peers both literally and figuratively scaffolded her learning and growth.

I once visited a class whose project focus was on building. The children had talked about construction, looked at books about building, practiced using tools at the woodworking bench, and visited construction sites. After much research, the children drew up their own blueprints for a playhouse in their yard. The day I visited, they were working on roofing. I observed as the children, with help from their teachers, climbed onto scaffolding and began to hammer shingles onto the roof. One little girl, Margaret, lingered around the construction site. She wanted to hammer nails. Judy, her teacher, said, "We are roofing today. If you would like to help, I can help you climb onto the scaffolding."

Margaret said, "No, I just want to hammer nails."

Judy was firm. "When you go back inside, you can use the woodworking bench, if you like. Right now we are roofing. If you don't want to help, there are many other choices."

I was troubled by this. My own training made me question this teacher's approach. It seemed rigid to me. I thought, *Why can't she just give the child a piece of wood, a hammer, and some nails? She could sit near the building project and hammer her nails.* My initial response was to compare the teacher's words to instructions from teachers in days of old who told the kids to draw a tree and added, "Color the leaves green, the trunk brown, and the sky blue." I didn't get it. I continued to watch the roofers as they hammered away.

Now and then Judy dropped a comment such as "Yesterday Peter was afraid to climb up on the scaffolding. He thought he couldn't hold on and hammer too." Margaret didn't budge from her spot, though there were many interesting choices available in the yard. She continued to watch the roofers. Judy continued to watch her.

Chapter 8

"When Ashanti first climbed up to work on the roof, she just watched for a while because she was so scared of being up high that she couldn't concentrate on hammering too," Judy said quietly after a while. I noticed that Margaret's initial whining and tearfulness at being prevented from hammering had stopped. She was now intently watching the roofers, who received periodic encouragement from their teacher.

"You're getting many shingles hammered in," Judy said. Margaret watched.

"I wonder," Judy finally said, "if Ashanti would hold your hand for a while to help you get used to being up high. Then maybe tomorrow you would feel like hammering too."

At this comment, Ashanti joined in, "C'mon, Margaret. I'll hold your hand. I was scared too before." Margaret stood up. Judy offered her assistance as Margaret climbed up the scaffolding. Ashanti held her hand once she got up. The look on her face changed from the sad, tentative, and displeased expressions she had worn all morning to one of utter triumph.

Overwhelmed by her accomplishment, Margaret's sense of competence exploded. "Gimme some nails!" she shouted joyfully. Margaret hammered her first shingle. Judy smiled. "A job well done!" she said. I learned a lot that day. I realized that, had I been Margaret's teacher, she'd have spent her morning happily on the edges of the building project. I'd have given her some nails, a board, and a hammer. She'd have been content to spend her time doing something she was comfortable with, without risking any new learning. At the end of the day, the child would have gone home much as she had arrived in the morning. Judy, however, sent home someone who had triumphed over fear, someone who had increased her skills and competence, which led to an increase in self-esteem. She had carefully observed her student and accurately judged that she was ready to take a leap with a little help. This is what Vygotsky meant by scaffolding. The skill of climbing the scaffold and hammering in the nails was within Margaret's ZPD. She wouldn't have done it on her own, but with help, she was able to achieve it.

It's important to recognize that using Vygotsky's ZPD requires careful observation of children and good judgment about how best to support their learning. Judy knew that Margaret was capable of doing the climbing and roofing. She knew that Margaret was afraid of being up high. She knew that Margaret would not choose to climb the scaffolding without help. All these observations and the resulting knowledge of the individual child are crucial to the successful scaffolding we see in this story. Without knowing each child well and taking the time for careful observation and reflection before urging a child further, teachers can make serious mistakes.

Language Development and Learning

Vygotsky believed that language presents the shared experience necessary for building cognitive development. He believed that talking is necessary to clarify important points and that talking with others helps us learn more about communication. We can learn much from observing children's conversations. It can help us find out what the children know and what they are confused about. Many of us have memories of schools where we were expected to be quiet and study. Teachers at the time thought learning was a solitary journey, something each student had to do alone. Vygotsky has shown us the importance of learning as an interactive experience. Teachers who want to encourage cognitive development can do it by encouraging conversations.

Sometimes teachers still discourage conversation. Often this happens at group time. Teachers do presentations on topics such as growing things, dinosaurs, or transportation, hoping to share their knowledge of the world with children. Interruptions are considered a disruption to the lesson. An understanding of Vygotsky's theory allows us to see the role of language (questioning, talking, joking, interrupting) in extending children's learning. In dramatic play, we frequently hear children adjusting their view of the world. For example, one day I overheard this conversation at a child care center:

> Juan: "I'll be the nurse."
> Nicole: "No, you can't! My mama's a nurse. You have to be a girl."
> Heather: "Yeah, the boys is supposed to be the doctors."
> Erleen: "The doctor that got my mom's baby out was a girl."
> Dylan: "C'mon, Juan, just be a doctor so we can play this game!"

Individual opinions are offered here. Experiences are shared. Dylan is even sophisticated enough to see that he and Juan are caught in a "word battle," and it's holding up the play. In this situation, there is content learning (people of all genders can be doctors) but also process learning (all this talking is getting in the way of play, but if we just agree, the play will go on).

Many teachers would have cut this discussion short by jumping in at the first incorrect statement to make sure the children knew that anyone can be a nurse. In the above situation, the teacher quietly concluded for the children as the conversation ended that it sounded as though they all knew different things about doctors and nurses but that it was true that people of any gender could work either job. By letting the children continue their arguments and discussions, she nurtured not only the content of the conversation but also the process that would help them all become better learners.

Social Interaction

According to Vygotsky, interactive situations like the one described above allow children to stretch and grow mentally. Too often teachers have acted as though language and cognitive abilities develop with little help or direction. But growing and learning does not necessarily happen on its own. One teacher I knew from an earlier generation used to say, "The children will grow taller without my help but not smarter or kinder!" Teachers need to develop the skills of observing, questioning, and encouraging peer interactions that best support children's growth and development. They need to think about when to step in with suggestions or ideas and when to let the children proceed on their own.

Vygotsky's theory that development is interactive changes the way we think about children's learning. For some teachers, the idea that children can help each other learn is very freeing. They suspect that they have sometimes interrupted excellent opportunities for group learning to call children to circle time, where they must sit and listen. Vygotsky has helped teachers to see that children learn not only by doing but also by talking, working with friends, and persisting at a task until they get it. To support children's social learning, teachers can provide many opportunities for children to help one another or to work together on projects of their choice.

I saw a fine example of this one spring day in northern New Hampshire. The rural Head Start program I was observing had a wonderful outdoor play area. Nature had provided a perfect science center. Shady areas offered patches of ice for sliding. Sunny areas offered muddy puddles of melted snow. Long icicles hung dripping from the building's low roof. Children played in every corner of the yard. Amid all this activity, two four-year-old boys found a treasure. Sticking out of some ice was the top of a mitten. They decided to excavate for the other half. First they tried digging with twigs. After large, small, and medium-size twigs had broken, they decided they needed "real" tools. The teacher unlocked a toolshed for them and observed their choice of tools. The boys brought out a shovel that was eighteen or twenty inches taller than either of them.

"It's stuck in there hard, so we need something big to get it out," Kevin said.

"Yup," Jeffrey agreed.

The teacher did not say, "That's too big," or "Someone will get

Chapter 8

hurt." She stayed nearby and watched. First the boys argued about who should dig first. Then Jeffrey, predictably, knocked the handle into Kevin when he tried to use the shovel.

"Let me," Kevin said. "You're not doing it right. You keep hitting me and not the mitten." Kevin tried—with the same outcome, of course.

The teacher said, "Wow, you guys are really working on that project."

The boys grinned but said, "It's not going right. Maybe we need a smaller digger."

The teacher said "Hmm, maybe so."

So off they went, returning with a small gardening rake and shovel. These boys sustained their focus and energy on this task for about half an hour. They got frustrated and talked out loud to each other and to themselves as they struggled. Eventually they got past taking turns and progressed to cooperation. They realized that one needed to dig while the other pulled.

When they finally got the mitten out, the wise teacher did not respond, "Good job." Instead, she offered, "You two worked really hard together. You tried many things. Some didn't work, but you didn't let yourselves feel discouraged. You kept trying other solutions. Together you worked it out. You must feel pleased with yourselves." This response to the children crystallized their experience and helped them understand it better by reflecting it back to them concretely and explicitly. This is another example of scaffolding.

The teacher boosted the children's learning by not rushing in to give them answers. Through interaction, conversation, and experimentation, the children increased their skills and accomplished their goals. They learned both process (how to negotiate about using tools, how to experiment to see which tool works the best) and content (what's the most effective way to dig a frozen object out of a patch of ice and, incidentally, principles of physics such as leverage) through their interactions. Vygotsky believed that learning and development are similar but not identical. The combination of instructing the child and honoring the child's individual development optimizes learning.

Executive Function

Evidence continues to mount that a preschool-age child's ability to apply cognitive control, also called executive function, is a better predictor of later school success than any academic learning acquired during the preschool years. Executive function encompasses self-regulation skills, including social skills, self-discipline, and mental flexibility. Children who lack these skills, or mental tools, do not know how to learn in a deliberate manner—they are "unable to focus their minds on purpose, and consequently their learning is less effective and efficient" (Bodrova and Leong 2007, 5).

Once, it was generally assumed these skills were ones not easily taught in the early childhood classroom. However, findings in brain research have established relationships between the development of self-regulation skills and the maturation of particular areas of the brain. The research suggests that as with many brain capacities, executive function can be built through practice. In addition, research shows that children develop the foundational skills for self-regulation in the first five years of life. These findings have many implications for early childhood education, and highlight the important role teachers play in helping young children develop the critical skills associated with executive function.

Two of Vygotsky's concepts are thought to be especially helpful in fostering self-regulation skills among young children: the zone of proximal development and scaffolding. Because self-regulation skills develop over time, it is important that teachers keep in mind each child's ZPD and offer learning experiences that are in keeping with what each child is ready to learn (scaffolding), including experiences the child can practice with teachers and able peers. Teaching techniques that foster self-regulation skills include modeling appropriate behavior and providing hints and cues about how and when children

Chapter 8

should regulate their behavior. Only after a child has consistently demonstrated self-regulation skills on his or her own, or has internalized those skills, should teachers begin withdrawing support.

While much is known about the positive effects of make-believe play on children's social, early literacy, and early mathematical development, research has shown that make-believe play also has positive effects on the development of self-regulation skills in young children. Inherent in make-believe play is the ZPD, because it is during this type of social play that children frequently behave beyond their years and their everyday behavior. As children participate in make-believe play, they are practicing regulating behavior naturally—they regulate other children by telling them what to do; they regulate themselves by staying in their roles and trying not to do anything that might interrupt the flow of the play; and they are regulated by other children when they agree to roles and rules that may not be the ones they had in mind.

Here's a great example of this. It's Deerfield Fair week in New Hampshire. RVs, campers, horse trailers, and trucks pull into the fairground. School closes on Friday, as experience has taught the superintendent that nobody comes that day anyway. Everyone is at the fair.

When the children return to school on Monday, the teacher has transformed the dramatic play area into a campsite at the fair. The children are ecstatic and begin at once to process and relive their weekend experiences. Josh (age six), Pete (four and a half), Heather (five), and Lynn (five and a half) are in the area together. Heather and Lynn immediately head to the stove and start pulling out a huge variety of "vegetables" to cook. The girls feel a sense of social dominance over food preparation. Josh, self-assured and clearly full of ideas, starts laying some ground rules. "First," he says, "we need to decide who we are. We need to be married. I'll be married to you, Heather."

Heather thinks this is wrong. All the children know each other's ages. "I should be married to Pete," she says (probably because they are close in age).

"No," Josh says. "She [Lynn] is the right size for Pete." (Lynn is older but smaller than Heather.) Josh is really into the play. He turns from the girls to Pete. "Didja bring the beer?" he says, comfortably.

Pete giggles and shakes his head. He looks at the teacher. He thinks he's probably not supposed to talk about beer at preschool.

Lynn, content to be part of the group, says nothing at all.

We can see the interactive nature Vygotsky describes in the children's play. Josh knows what to do immediately. He never questions the appropriateness of his words, as they are supposed to be adults at the fair. Heather rejects her suggested role, as she concludes age, not height, should make the match. Pete's behavior is a good indicator of self-regulation at work. He senses *beer* is not a school word, but he isn't quite sure. He's not as confident of his role in the play as Josh is. Lynn listens as her eyes dart from one to the other of her peers. She is quiet, not comfortable speaking up in the setting, yet confident enough to do just what she wants to—enjoy watching and learning from the rest of her peers.

Teachers who want to apply Vygotsky's ideas about the ZPD and scaffolding to encourage rich make-believe play in their early childhood programs can do these things:

- ensure children have enough time for play
- offer children appropriate toys and props
- observe children's play and, when appropriate, share ideas for themes that could enrich and extend their play

Vygotsky in the Twenty-First Century

Vygotsky added a new voice to those of his peers when he suggested that interaction is as important to learning as constructing one's own ideas. His zone of proximal development was a startling addition to those of us taught a purely Piagetian approach to young children and learning. There was great emphasis for at least three decades (1960s, 1970s, and 1980s) on the importance of *not* pushing preschoolers. Initially the notion of ZPG and taking children to the next possible step created an instinctive (or conditioned) cringe. We didn't want to push!

But it makes sense, and the idea took some pressure off us by suggesting that children often learn as much or more from a more skilled peer than they do from their teachers. As we all tried to scaffold children's learning, we realized these ideas really do work. Then again, the pace of many preschool and primary grades these days doesn't leave much time for teachers to encourage conversation.

Given what we know from Vygotsky about executive function's impact on self-regulation, it is frustrating that school districts are discouraging play and conversation in kindergarten in favor of drilling in academics. We know from many experiences that the guidance of our founding theorists is as important today as it was when they first laid out these ideas. So what are committed educators to do with the gaps between what we know is best and what is expected from us?

I suggest that every parent and teacher interested in the future of our society and education read Jonathan Haidt's 2024 book *The Anxious Generation*. This will not be a comforting read in light of Vygotsky's work, as Haidt suggests that young children growing up on screens and social media platforms are less competent at verbal interaction than the children of many previous generations were. We cannot look progress in the face, judge it as detrimental, and turn the other way. But Haidt's book gives us one more sobering piece of information to contemplate so that together we can all begin developing strategies to help young children interact with and learn from one another.

Discussion Questions

1. When your school district implements a K–3 primary program, some parents are upset that younger children will "hold

back" the learning of their second and third graders. Using Vygotsky's sociocultural theory of development, tell parents how the new program will be good for all the children.

2. Kimberly is a five-year-old in your preschool. Her parents want her to read before entering first grade. You've read David Elkind. He says, "Don't push children." You've read Vygotsky. He says if reading is in a child's ZPD, it's okay to push a little. You've read Piaget. He says play is the best way for children to learn. You have to decide how to work with Kimberly's family to help her make the transition to public school. What do you need to know about Kimberly before you decide what to do? What are some possible ways of handling the situation? How would you choose one?

3. Many primary-grade classrooms expect children not to socialize with other children during their class time. What would Vygotsky think of this practice? Why?

Suggestions for Further Reading

Barrs, Myra. 2022. *Vygotsky the Teacher: A Companion to His Psychology for Teachers and Other Practitioners*. Routledge.

Berk, Laura E., and Adam Winsler. 1995. *Scaffolding Children's Learning: Vygotsky and Early Childhood Education*. National Association for the Education of Young Children.

Galinsky, Ellen. 2010. *Mind in the Making: The Seven Essential Life Skills Every Child Needs*. HarperCollins.

Karpov, Yuriy. 2014. *Vygotsky for Educators*. Cambridge University Press.

Vygotsky, Lev. 1978. *Mind in Society: The Development of Higher Psychological Processes*. Harvard University Press.

Chapter 9: Janice E. Hale

The educational problem presented becomes a matter of providing educational resources to develop maximally the abilities of all ethnic groups even at the expense of magnifying the differences between the groups. The orientation of most education research is to minimize, decrease, or ignore the differences between groups so that education can proceed more easily and economically.

—**Janice E. Hale**, *Black Children*

Biography

BORN IN 1948, JANICE HALE was a practicing professor of early childhood education at Wayne State University in Detroit, Michigan. She was an educator, researcher, and mother with a research focus on Black children and the support they require within a school setting. She spent her career researching early childhood education with a focus on creating educational excellence for Black children. She founded the demonstration school Visions for Children, which was designed to facilitate the intellectual development of Black preschool children. She received her bachelor's degree in sociology and elementary education from Spelman College, a master's degree in religious education from the Interdenominational Theological Center in Atlanta, and a doctorate in early childhood education from Georgia State University.

With the belief that initiatives for improving education for Black children were not enough, she created a framework that outlined strategies for schools and leaders. Hale redefined schools' responsibilities in creating a community for Black and Brown learners that expanded beyond the school's walls. With passion for the field and for supporting marginalized communities, Hale called upon educators to give up their belief that educational limitations of Black children are the reasons for the achievement gap and to recognize that each child is too precious to be left behind. Hale was a "committed scholar and activist for the right of Black children to education" (Gardner et al. 2020, 73) and paved the way for other educators and researchers.

Many of the theorists discussed in this book have influenced educators in their understanding of children's learning and development in predominantly White educational settings, which occupy the default norm in society today. In his article "Black Skin, White Theorists: Remembering Hidden Black Early Childhood Scholars," Anthony Broughton (2020) highlights the exclusion of Black scholars in educational settings. He notes how he personally had to analyze his own early childhood development through a White theoretical lens due to the prominence of White voices in early childhood development theory. Broughton, a Black male educator, believes it essential to highlight "Black intellectual thoughts that explore multiple ways of knowing and being a Black child through a Black lens." When examining Black scholars in the field, he discusses the foundational research Hale brought to the field of ECE and notes that her work "remains relevant in a field that still ignores the contributions of African American leaders and applies conventional child development theories to all children."

Hale's Theory

Hale calls on educators to be informed of their students' cultural contexts and experiences. Barbara Bowman and coauthors (2018, 17) define culture as "what groups create over time to adapt to their environment; it determines to a large extent how adults interact with children." They explain how as "parents adapt to different environmental challenges, they develop different child-rearing strategies, many of which are misunderstood by those unfamiliar with a community's history." Black children are raised at home and in communities that at times prove incompatible with school culture (Bowman et al. 2018; Hale 1986; Hale 2001). Teachers who understand Black history (slavery, segregation, and the continued injustices Black people experience today) can better understand Black children's behavior. For example, as a result of the Atlantic slave trade, Black people in the United States combined their home languages with English to create a language to converse with one another. The remnants continue today as Black American English (Bowman et al. 2018, Frieson and Presiado 2022). At the same time, Black languages and literacies have been perceived as deficient for centuries, as the United States has a lengthy history of grappling with providing meaningful educational experiences for Black children (Muhammad 2020). In support of Hale's call to educators, Bowman and colleagues (2018, 18) emphasize:

> The African American culture transmitted from generation to generation needs to be understood as rich and noteworthy and needs to be used as the entry to new skills and knowledge. By recognizing the meaning and value of children's home knowledge, teachers can use home culture as a foundation from which to extend children's thinking rather than considering it an impediment.

School is placed at the center of Hale's work to achieve upward mobility for Black children because everyone is required to go to school. Her model of culturally appropriate pedagogy, which is referred to today as pro-Black pedagogy, focuses on learning styles and instructional strategies for use with children in preschool and elementary school (Muller et al. 2022, 566). Hale suggests a model with three components to support Black students developmentally and academically:

Chapter 9

- classroom instruction
- instructional accountability infrastructure
- cultural enrichment

Classroom Instruction

In much of Hale's research, the focus is improving education for Black children. In her model to support Black students, she begins with classroom instruction as the focal point. Hale recognized three purposes for educating children: imparting skills, creating experiences and opportunities for real world exposure, and providing children with opportunities to develop talents and interests.

Describing her vision for classroom instruction, she says, "A process of education must be crafted that motivates African American children to regard academic activities as interesting and fun" (Hale 2001, 114). In the late twentieth century, leading into the twenty-first, Hale noted the disparity in academic achievement between Black children and their White peers. This disparity continues today with Black children, on average, scoring lower on tests and given lower grades than other demographics of students (Asian, White, and Latino) (Bowman et al. 2018; Hale 2016; Muller et al. 2022).

Hale encourages educators to examine the cultures of students so they can teach to the strengths of the environments children come from. For example, Hale notes that "African American culture has a strong orientation toward oral communication, whereas the dominant culture is oriented toward literacy" (Hale 2001, 119). Dr. Gloria Boutte and Dr. Kim Parker encourage educators to uphold and recognize the culture and histories of Black children, noting, "Many Black children are proficient with stylistic literacies, communicating in ways that are different. Orality is important in Black culture, and so it's amazing to me that Black children come to school, and teachers don't see these literacies because they're not in conventional form" (Gardner et al. 2020, 74). Hale's research on Black culture,

African history, and their impact on Black children informed her recommendations for instructional practices within the classroom. Hale believed Black children learn best when their learning is oriented toward people rather than objects. They respond best when they are instructed in small, nurturing groups with a great deal of interaction between child and teacher and child and peers.

As Hale (2001, 122) emphasized,

> A model of classroom instruction for African American children should diminish the use of xeroxed worksheets, workbooks, textbooks, and a skill-and-drill orientation. Emphasis should be placed instead on hands-on activities, projects, interrelated learning experiences, field trips, speakers, and classroom visitors. The intent is to create a learning environment that complements the culture of the African American community and stimulates higher-order thinking and creativity among African American children.

Bowman and coauthors (2018, 20) warn us that "too often, teachers and administrators view the different expressions of development in African Americans as evidence of intentionally bad and distasteful behavior and/or low academic potential." The education of early childhood teachers is essential to narrowing the achievement gap among students. When teachers use effective engagement methods, Black children can achieve the same academic and social development in school as their peers (Bowman et al. 2018). Bowman encourages preparatory institutions and professional development programs to prepare educators to understand that child development and learning are linked and focus on how to facilitate learning for children from various backgrounds.

One way to support students in educational settings is to examine class sizes and ratios. Hale's findings suggest that large class sizes with high teacher-student ratios, as found in most urban school districts, are barriers to the achievement of Black children. Hale (2001, 119) refers to the National Association for the Education of Young Children (NAEYC) to make the following recommendations:

1. for four-to five-year-olds, a ratio of two adults to no more than twenty children

2. for six-, seven-, and eight-year-olds, a ratio of no more than twenty-five children to two adults, one of whom may be a paraprofessional, and no more than eighteen children to one professional teacher

3. grouping children whose ages span two or three chronological ages, while providing flexibility for students to be instructed at their individual learning and growth levels

To aid in having smaller ratios of children to adults, Hale recommends inviting parents and community volunteers to work with children. Having more adults present reduces the time the educator spends teaching the whole class at once, and it allows teachers to work more with children in smaller groups. She also recommends involving churches as a resource of mentorship for students.

NAEYC emphasizes the importance of incorporating pro-Black curriculum at an early age. While having a range of ethnic, cultural, and linguistic groups represented in early years learning experiences is noted as important, NAEYC's guidelines also encourage educators to incorporate lessons with a specific focus on African, African Diaspora, and African American contributions to the world's knowledge. The goal is for teachers to broaden White-dominant curricula by normalizing Black joy. LaGarrett J. King (2020, 338) noted in his research on Black history that Black joy is "the love, collegiality, and collectiveness that Black people have exhibited throughout history" and the accomplishment, agency, and resistance of Black people.

Instructional Accountability Infrastructure

To ensure Black children's needs are met both developmentally and instructionally, Hale (2001, 138) believes leaders and principals "can make the difference in whether children succeed, fail with retention, or fail with social promotion."

The instructional leader works with teachers to plan units of instruction, observes teachers on a regular basis, and then meets with teachers for reflection and feedback. It is the role of the leader to monitor the outcomes for children and identify anyone who may be falling through the cracks. Teachers beginning their careers right out of college face a steep learning curve. Despite the degrees they have, they need guidance and mentorship to learn to support every student.

To increase culturally appropriate practices, Hale urges schools and administrators to create an accountability system that upholds instructional standards. The earlier in a child's education this type of system can be implemented the better. An accountability system has several components that all work together: community involvement, which often goes hand in hand with an in loco parentis ("in the place of parents") committee, all threaded through with the vision and mission upheld by program leadership.

Hale believes leadership must work with an in loco parentis committee composed of community members so that excellent instruction is delivered to all children. Hale recommends the committee be composed of the age-level teacher, a volunteer from the community, and a parent representative. The committee provides educators with instructional support through practices such as recruiting community members to work with children in small groups, creating a peer evaluation system for teaching and best practices (where exemplar and experienced teachers work with new educators), involving parents during in-service training, and encouraging older children to donate time to work with younger children. The in loco parentis committee provides an additional component of accountability to monitor children's progress and provide the support each child needs to perform at grade level. Through regular meetings with the classroom teacher, the committee can consider who is not performing at grade level and determine who might benefit from private tutoring, counseling, or alternative instruction strategies. Necessary training and support would be provided for those willing to participate in this committee. Hale (2001, 142) proposes this committee would "create an academic safety net for every child in the school. Any child in this school is in 'the Family' and will not be left behind." The younger the children are, the more benefit they gain when extra adults work with them. Collaborating with Black communities and welcoming families into schools elevates student growth and performance.

Hale believes leaders can create instructional accountability by encouraging collaboration between teachers and administrators when lesson planning; holding principal-led observations with debrief reflection meetings after; and providing resources to improve areas of instructional challenge. In accordance with Hale, Lisa Ranfos, the executive director at the lab school at the University of New Hampshire, describes a process in which teachers beginning their career go through a year of mentorship to "give them the tools they need in their toolbox" (Ranfos 2024). This mentorship prepares them to teach independently. Teachers set goals, and continued meetings throughout the year between teacher and leader create the infrastructure needed to ensure children are getting the supports they need. Ranfos recommends using video reflections with new teachers so teachers watch their instruction and reflect with an experienced educator. This mentorship process provides an opportunity for leaders to help build on teachers' strengths, thus making these new educators comfortable and confident in their skills.

Cultural Enrichment

Hale stresses how cultural enrichment provides opportunities for children to connect to their future goals and success. Extracurricular, enrichment, and cultural activities play a large part in the discovery and development of children's talents and interests, motivating students' learning and expanding their opportunities while also including families and community resources. As Hale (2001, 143) emphasizes,

> The arena of human activity that enables children to develop social and political skills, to identify talents and interests that can lead to satisfying leisure time activities and careers, and to find meaning in their daily lives does not come from the activities that children engage in in the classroom—at least not in the classrooms that serve inner-city African American children. These skills are developed through enriching activities outside the classroom.

Activities such as choice opportunities, male mentorship, and parent-organized cultural excursions are options for this cultural enrichment component of Hale's model. Hale leans on leadership (principals or superintendents) to reach out to the community to identify men who would serve as mentors to individual boys. She recommends providing space for social gatherings for male mentors and mentees. Hale encourages parents to provide cultural activities for students. She gives the example of having a family member who is skilled in piano come to the school and provide music lessons for students. Hale recommends forming a committee composed of volunteers to network within the school and community to provide experiences that will enrich children's lives and broaden their exposure to different settings and opportunities.

Providing children with choice strengthens their interests and intrinsic motivation as well as connecting them to academic achievement. Hale notes a school in Michigan that provides free choice to children beginning at the age of three. At first children are provided specific times to select activities that will strengthen their interest in creative and academic activities, such as painting, puzzles, or dramatic play. By the time children are seven, they are signing up for ten-week courses of choice that focus on different areas of sports and movement, performing arts and visual arts, and STEM (science, technology, engineering, and math).

Colleen McKinnon, a Black principal at an early primary school in Brooklyn, New York, builds on Hale's idea of parent-organized cultural excursions by combining community with enrichment, bringing in Black artists and family members from the community to teach students about visual arts and dance. Additionally, McKinnon invites community members and organizations to the school to provide enrichment programs and opportunities ranging from sharing heart health information to leading mural painting and drumming tutorials.

During an interview, McKinnon, a graduate of Spelman College like Hale, discussed the enthusiasm she felt as a student at a historically Black college who was encouraged to embrace her Black identity. McKinnon related her experiences learning Black history and growing her pride in her lineage while also understanding the more painful aspects of that history. As a leader, she believes it is her duty to build these experiences with her students from an early age. She notes, "We don't focus on building pride because students come with a lot of pride in themselves, but we continue to foster that pride. We create opportunities where they can showcase all that we love about who they are, and about their history, and about their culture. And so it is a focus from the very beginning" (McKinnon 2024).

McKinnon focuses on the theme of Black excellence, which can be defined as "achievement in scholarship, service, and leadership as acknowledged by peers, parents, and other members of the Black community who are making a difference" (Scott 2017, 111). While discussing preparing for a new school year, McKinnon (2024) notes, "If Black excellence is our end goal, how does that show up? How can we bring that into our school?" She uses the example of the Divine Nine sororities and fraternities, which have chapters at the historically Black colleges and universities (HBCUs). She named each classroom after a different Divine Nine sorority or fraternity and educated the students on the differences among the chapters to celebrate the excellence that each one brings. To McKinnon, associating the classrooms with Black excellence, such as the Divine Nine, provides critical representation and inspiration to young children.

Hale in the Twenty-First Century

In 2019 NAEYC drafted a practice position statement highlighting ways in which Western perspectives have been dominant in early childhood readings and conversation. The statement challenged universalistic views of child development by recognizing the nuances of the various contexts that shape children's ways of being. The NAEYC position statement is "inclusive of multi-ethnic perspectives, which provides a deeper context to what is known as child development" (Broughton 2020). In describing the research behind the statement, its authors note that all child development and learning are affected by social and cultural contexts, and that social and cultural aspects

> provide the framework for all development and learning. For example, play is a universal phenomenon across all cultures (it also extends to other primates). Play, however, can vary significantly by social and cultural contexts as children use play as a means of interpreting and making sense of their experiences. Early childhood educators need to understand the commonalities of children's development and learning and how those commonalities take unique forms as they reflect the social and cultural frameworks in which they occur (NAEYC 2020, 6).

Chapter 9

There are many examples in research that illustrate how children start to notice differences and begin to classify and categorize. Between ages three and five, they can draw conclusions about aspects of their identity, such as race (Derman-Sparks 2008). Thus, the work of the early childhood teacher is critically important. Young children recognize race and cannot avoid absorbing messages of White superiority because anti-Blackness is the most dominant form of racism in the United States. As educators, we have a responsibility to counter these anti-Black messages and teach in pro-Black ways. It is important to note that "pro-Black does not mean anti-white or anti-other ethnic groups. It simply declares an unapologetic, positive, proactive perspective regarding Blackness and Black people" (Muller et al. 2022).

As Hale notes, "The Black community has been engaged in a struggle to see their experiences, history, and lifestyle reflected in the education children receive" (Hale 1986, 157). Dr. Gloria Boutte, a professor at the University of South Carolina, has spent years researching and teaching about structural forms that uphold and recognize the culture and histories of Black children, focusing on representation and designing a pro-Black curriculum. Boutte's research has transformed teaching practices of thousands of teachers across the nation. Because she is a Black woman, Boutte's work is both personal and professional. Experiencing racial injustices both in her own education and in her daughters', Boutte believes using real-life scenarios is critical for bringing theory to life. At the beginning of Boutte's journey of research and education, Janice Hale served as a foundational model for her in focusing on the welfare of Black children in schools. Boutte's background is in child development, and she began her writing around Black children's development, culture, and language. She has worked to dismantle the harmful deficit narratives of Black children as "anti-intellectual, disengaged, or unable to succeed" (Gardner et al. 2020, 74).

Here are a few actions educators can take to incorporate a more pro-Black curriculum:

- Challenge Eurocentric curricula by including as many books about Africans and people of African descent as there are about Europeans and European Americans.

- Require rich representations of Blackness in computer programs, songs, and music.

- Include Black artists, inventors, and scientists at construction, art, and science centers.

At the Early Childhood Education Assembly, the National Council of Teachers of English emphasized the importance of bringing race into early learning, noting, "Conversations about race and racism and teaching racial histories can and must happen with youngest children if they are to grow into adults who will create more equitable tomorrows" (Muller et al. 2022). As educators of young children, it is essential that we have discourse around pro-Black pedagogy and begin to implement strategies in the classroom.

Discussion Questions

1. Take an inventory of your practices and curriculum. How can you intentionally build children's understanding of Black joy? In what ways can this knowledge be a foundational part of students' early childhood experience?

2. It's the beginning of the school year and you want to include families as part of the learning community within your program. What efforts can you make to collaborate with both your colleagues and children's families to institute this?

3. In what ways can families be involved in discussions about race and pro-Black pedagogy?

Chapter 9

Suggestions for Further Reading

Boutte, Gloria Swindler, and Kamania Wynter-Hoyte. 2023. *Revolutionary Love for Early Childhood Classrooms: Nurturing the Brilliance of Young Black Children*. Scholastic.

Iruka, Iheoma, Stephanie Curenton, and Tonia Durden. 2020. *Don't Look Away: Embracing Anti-Bias Classrooms*. Gryphon House.

Sturdivant, Toni. 2023. *I Like Myself: Fostering Positive Racial Identity in Young Black Children*. Redleaf Press.

Sullivan, Debra Ren-Etta. 2016. *Cultivating the Genius of Black Children: Strategies to Close the Achievement Gap in the Early Years*. Redleaf Press.

Chapter 10: Putting Theory to Practice

WHAT ARE OUR PRACTICES? In its position paper on professional preparation standards, NAEYC (2009, 1) is clear: "Excellent teachers are decision makers, engaged in a continuous interplay of theory, research and practice." Sadly, because many children have teachers unfamiliar with ECE theories, many practices in ECE programs are not based on foundational theories.

In the context of ECE, the word *practice* means the planned activities we intend to offer children throughout their days and years with us. These usually include curriculum areas such as mathematics, physical education, music, dance, science, literacy, and art, adapted to the developmental ages and stages of the children we are teaching as well as their individual interests and abilities.

However, *practice* also means a way of responding to children throughout their days and years with us. This way of responding ideally includes consistent respect for the child and family, understanding of the child's temperament and individual preferences, understanding of the family's culture and preferences, and general knowledge of typical and atypical child growth and development. Our actions—indeed, our practices—as educators are informed by the kind of people we are, what we have learned, and where and how we have learned. Our practices come from the kind of people we have had as preschool and college teachers. Our practices come from our own temperaments. Some of us are active, loud, exuberant, funny, and compassionate. Some of us are quiet, reflective, cautious, conservative, and compassionate.

In my earlier discussions with teachers about theories versus practice, I loved the comment "We are still practicing at our practices." This statement applies to teachers at every level, because in order to include all of these elements (including decision making and the interplay of theory, research, and practice) in one's approach to daily practice, a teacher needs thorough knowledge of theory through high-quality postsecondary education, good mentors to help put the pieces together, excellent supervision, and time for reflection on all of these pieces, both alone and in the company of coteachers.

When I reflect on my conversations with teachers, I am particularly struck by comments like "Developmentally appropriate practice (DAP) is a theory, but fingerpainting is a practice." For well-trained teachers who understand the foundational theories, *both* are *both*. DAP is a theory that becomes a practice, just as fingerpainting is a practice that is understood through theory. A well-informed and prepared teacher would say something like "We have many children that have much to cope with in their young lives, so we try to offer fingerpainting on a regular basis. It is such a wonderful activity to relieve tension. We devote a good part of our budget each year to making sure we offer frequent and rich experiences with this medium."

This brief description of the theoretical reasons for practicing fingerpainting with young children tells us much about this teacher's understanding of both young children and of curriculum:

- They know the children and families they are working with.

- They are aware of children's and families' stresses.

- They understand that coping skills are primitive in most three-year-olds and that young children need appropriate outlets for their stress.

- They know that fingerpainting is both an art form (free, beautiful, interesting, and undefined) as well as therapeutic (as a messy, tactile, squishy, direct sensory experience).

- They have learned that the experience is rich and relaxing when quantities and thickness of paint are carefully considered.

This teacher is "practicing" DAP, and their knowledge of the child and the benefits of fingerpainting weave theory and practice together beautifully, thus making it a fine example of what we can consider theories *of* practice. It is important to consider that such weaving of theories of practice requires knowledge and understanding of children, development, and curriculum. This example would not separate theory (DAP) and practice (fingerpainting) but make them one and the same.

Now think of a teacher who does not understand the impact of stress on young children. They don't know any tension-relieving activities or high-quality art experiences for young children. They set out fingerpainting three times a week because the director wants them to do so. This is an example of practice without accompanying theory.

As the studies cited earlier make clear, it is the early childhood–specific training of the first teacher that makes the fingerpainting a high-quality experience for children. The second teacher is doing as they are told. They set out the activity three times a week, but that task could as easily be done by the custodian, the cook, or a parent volunteer. The first teacher is intentional in their choice for the child. They know from their education that their planned activity is responding to a particular child's need. They would not urge all the children to paint—they would know that the child in need would automatically choose to do it. The children who are not interested or don't like the paint on their fingers are free to make a different choice.

Beginning with the National Day Care Study in 1979 (Ruopp et al 1979), followed by credible studies that concur with those findings (Feeney 2012; Goffin 2013), research evidence has made it clear that a few specific elements are common to most programs offering high-quality care:

- small group size
- low ratio of adult caregivers to children

Chapter 10

- early childhood–specific education of caregivers

The fact that these findings have been repeatedly duplicated implies that early childhood–*specific* education is a huge predictor of a high-quality program.

For many years, when posting desirable jobs, I included the language "ECE training and experience required." Initially office support staff asked if I thought I should write out what *ECE* stands for. My answer was always no. I was not looking for candidates who didn't know what ECE stood for. Additionally, I would quickly hire a candidate with an associate's degree in ECE over an applicant with a master's degree in anything else. Knowing how children grow and react to a variety of circumstances is critical to being able to adequately nurture their learning and development.

In the ECE field, there is a discrepancy between the widespread knowledge that early childhood–specific education is an indicator of high-quality programming and the fact that many in the field avoid requiring that education in the workforce. It is the elephant in the room that no one mentions. We need to have more frequent, honest, and respectful conversations about this matter. Loving and enjoying children is essential to working with them, *and* professional training is equally important. Too often our field has used an either/or rather than a both/and context for looking at teacher credentials. Educator Herbert Kohl (1984, 16) was right over forty years ago when he wrote, "With the rarest exceptions, one has to learn how to become a good teacher just as one has to learn how to become a scientist or an artist." Teaching is a learned art, and we must recognize it as such within our field.

Decades ago, the child care system was not as developed as it is today. The research on children's early brain development has done much to convince all of us that developmental needs must be taken seriously from conception on. Infant and toddler care is as important as, if not more important than, the preschool years. Yet frequently members of the public are unaware of the critical learning that takes place all day every day for young children. This lack of understanding is so widespread that it reaches right into the ECE workplace. Many directors have told me that they have difficulty staffing the infant room because staff say they want to "really" teach. I have had similar experiences myself.

Daphna Bassok and her colleagues (2013, 583) claim, "The few studies that have examined the evolution of the ECE workforce over time actually suggest that the qualifications of the workforce have either changed only modestly or have declined." If the average child care center employee has only a high school diploma or, at best, an associate's degree, it is unlikely that they would have the know-how to create the learning environment or experiences for children that a certified teacher with a degree in ECE provides in a public school pre-K or kindergarten. This does not necessarily mean the child care center is poor quality, and it does not make the provider a bad person, but the data show that we will recognize the difference when we walk into those two classrooms. For the good of all our children, we need more people with child development and education degrees teaching and caring for young children. When large numbers of the ECE workforce have no training past high school, how can we expect them to merge our foundational theories with their daily practice?

Teachers need to be familiar with educational terms and theories before they can practice them. If aspiring early educators do not understand the need to learn about these foundational theories or their relevance to daily practices with young children and their families and do not pursue them with seriousness of purpose, then perhaps they should pursue other lines of work. It is important to note here that it is quite possible for teachers to go through the process of getting a degree in ECE and still not make the necessary connections between theory and practice. My graduate school mentor used to say, "There are, of course, students who go through the program, but the program never quite goes through them." I find that those who oppose college requirements for ECE teachers tend to frequently use the rationale that just because someone goes to college doesn't guarantee that they will be a good teacher. That, of course, is true. But research demonstrates that the odds of becoming a good teacher are greatly increased by rigorous training in both child development and early education (Alvarado-Suarez and Acosta-Gonzalez 2022). Certainly teachers can study child development yet not apply this knowledge in their work with children. However, if teachers haven't studied at all, then it is luck or coincidence if they manage to make the best choices for children and their early education. Children deserve better.

References

Ainsworth, Mary D. Salter. 1967. *Infancy in Uganda: Infant Care and the Growth of Love*. Johns Hopkins University Press.

Allen, Brian. 2023. *The Science and Clinical Practice of Attachment Theory: A Guide from Infancy to Adulthood*. American Psychological Association.

Alvarado-Suarez, Martina A., and Hugo Nicolás Acosta-Gonzalez. 2022. "The Effects of an Early Childhood Education Care Program on Child Development as a Function of Length of Exposure in Ecuador." *International Journal of Educational Development* 89 (January): 102559.

Bassok, Daphna, Maria Fitzpatrick, Susanna Loeb, and Agustina S. Paglayan. 2013. "The Early Childhood Care and Education Workforce from 1990 through 2010: Changing Dynamics and Persistent Concerns." *Education Finance and Policy* 8 (4): 581–601.

Berger, Kathleen Stassen. 2001. *The Developing Person Through the Life Span*. Worth Publishers.

Bodrova, Elena, and Deborah J. Leong. 2007. *Tools of the Mind: The Vygotskian Approach to Early Childhood Education*. 2nd ed. Pearson Education, Inc.

Bowlby, John. 1940. "The Influence of Early Environment in the Development of Neurosis and Neurotic Character." *International Journal of Psychoanalysis* 21:154–78.

———. 1951. *Maternal Care and Mental Health*. World Health Organization Series (2).

———. 1958. *Can I Leave My Baby?* National Association for Mental Health.

———. 1970. *Child Care and the Growth of Love*. 2nd ed. Pelican.

———. 1973. *Attachment and Loss Volume 2: Separation*. Basic Books.

———. 1980. *Attachment and Loss Volume 3: Loss, Sadness and Depression*. Basic Books.

———. 1982. *Attachment and Loss Volume 1: Attachment*. Revised ed. Basic Books.

Bowman, Barbara, James Comer, and David Johns. 2018. "Addressing the African American Achievement Gap." *Young Children* 73, no. 2 (May): 14–23.

Brazelton, T. Berry. 1979. *Infants and Mothers: Differences in Development*. Delacorte Press.

———. 1981. *On Becoming a Family*. Delacorte Press.

———. 1985. *Working and Caring*. Addison-Wesley Publishing Company.

References

———. 1992. *Touchpoints: The Essential Reference: Your Child's Emotional and Behavioral Development.* Addison-Wesley Publishing Company.

Brazelton, T. Berry, and Joshua D. Sparrow. 2003. *Discipline: The Brazelton Way.* Perseus Publishing.

Bronfenbrenner, Urie. 1979. *The Ecology of Human Development.* Perseus Publishing.

Broughton, Anthony. 2020. "Black Skin, White Theorists: Remembering Hidden Black Early Childhood Scholars." *Contemporary Issues in Early Childhood* 23 (1). https://doi.org/10.1177/1463949120958101.

Chaillé, Christine, and Lory Britain. 2003. *The Young Child as Scientist: A Constructivist Approach to Early Childhood Science Education*, 3rd ed. Allyn and Bacon.

Chang, Hyein, Daniel S. Shaw, and JeeWon Cheong. 2015. "The Development of Emotional and Behavioral Control in Early Childhood: Heterotypic Continuity and Relations to Early School Adjustment." *Journal of Child and Adolescent Behavior* 3, no. 3 (May): 204.

Coontz, Stephanie. 2016. *The Way We Never Were: American Families and the Nostalgia Trap.* Basic Books.

Copple, Carol, and Natalie Cavanaugh 2003. *A World of Difference: Readings on Teaching Young Children in a Diverse Society.* National Association for the Education of Young Children.

Crittenden, Ann. 2001. *The Price of Motherhood: Why the Most Important Job in the World Is Still the Least Valued.* Henry Holt and Company.

Derman-Sparks, Louise. 2008. Keep On, Keeping On: Progress, Challenges and Possibilities for Anti-Bias Education. *International Journal of Equity and Innovation in Early Childhood* 6 (2): 3–13.

Dewey, John. 1897. *My Pedagogic Creed.* E. L. Kellogg and Company.

———. 1899. *The School and Society.* University of Chicago Press.

———. 1938. *Experience and Education.* Macmillan.

Douglas, Susan J., and Meredith W. Michaels. 2005. *The Mommy Myth: The Idealization of Motherhood and How It Has Undermined All Women.* Free Press.

Eisenberg, Nancy, Sandra Losoya, Ivanna K. Guthrie, et al. 2001. "Parental Socialization of Children's Dysregulated Expression of Emotion and Externalizing Problems." *Journal of Family Psychology* 15 (2): 183–205.

Erikson, Erik. 1968. *Identity: Youth and Crisis.* W. W. Norton & Company.

———. 1963 [1950]. *Childhood and Society.* W. W. Norton & Company.

Feeney, Stephanie. 2012. *Professionalism in Early Childhood Education: Doing Our Best for Young Children.* Pearson Education.

Fraiberg, Selma. 1977. *Every Child's Birthright.* Basic Books.

References

Frieson, Brittany L., and Vivian E. Presiado. 2022. "Supporting Multilingual Black Children: Building on Black Language Genius." *Reading Teacher* 75 (April): 707–15.

Gandini, Lella, and Carolyn Pope Edwards. 2001. *Bambini: The Italian Approach to Infant/Toddler Care*. Teachers College Press.

Gardner, Roberta Price, Eliza G. Braden, and Haeny Yoon. 2020. "We Be Lovin' Black Children: NCTE's 2020 Outstanding Elementary Educators in the English Language Arts." *Language Arts* 98 (2): 71–79.

Gesell, Arnold, and Frances L. Ilg. 1943. *Infant and Child in the Culture of Today*. Harper and Row.

Ginott, Haim G. 1969. *Between Parent and Teenager*. Macmillan.

Goffin, Stacie G. 2013. *Early Childhood Education for a New Era: Leading for Our Profession*. Teachers College Press.

Gonzalez-Mena, Janet. 1993. *Multicultural Issues in Child Care*. Mayfield Publishing Company.

Greenman, Jim, Anne Stonehouse, and Gigi Schweikert. 2008. *Prime Times*. Redleaf Press.

Haidt, Jonathan. 2024. *The Anxious Generation*. Penguin Press.

Hale, Janice E. 1986. *Black Children: Their Roots, Culture, and Learning Styles*. Revised ed. Johns Hopkins University Press.

———. 2001. *Learning While Black: Creating Educational Excellence for African American Children*. Johns Hopkins University Press.

———. 2016. "Thirty-Year Retrospective on the Learning Styles of African American Children." *Education and Urban Society* 48 (5): 444–59.

Halfon, Neal, Kathryn Taaffe McLearn, and Mark A. Schuster. 2002. *Child Rearing in America: Challenges Facing Parents of Young Children*. Cambridge University Press.

Harlow, Harry. 1958. "The Nature of Love." *American Psychologist* 13 (12): 673–85.

Hast, Fran, and Ann Hollyfield. 1999. *Infant and Toddler Experiences*. Redleaf Press.

Hendrick, Joanne. 1992. *The Whole Child: Development Education for the Early Years*. 5th ed. New York: Merrill.

Honig, Alice Sterling. 2002. *Secure Relationships: Nurturing Infant/Toddler Attachment in Early Care Settings*. National Association for the Education of Young Children.

Jervis, Kathe, ed. 1999. *Separation: Strategies for Helping Two- to Four-Year-Olds*. National Association for the Education of Young Children.

Johns Hopkins Center for Gun Violence Solutions. 2025. "Gun Violence in the United States 2023: Examining the Gun Suicide Epidemic." https://publichealth.jhu.edu/sites/default/files/2025-06/2023-cgvs-gun-violence-in-the-united-states.pdf.

References

Jones, Elizabeth. 1986. *Teaching Adults an Active Learning Approach*. National Association for the Education of Young Children.

Kagan, Jerome. 1998. *Three Seductive Ideas*. Harvard University Press.

Karen, Robert. 1998. *Becoming Attached: First Relationships and How They Shape Our Capacity to Love*. Oxford University Press.

Karr-Morse, Robin, and Meredith S. Wiley. 1997. *Ghosts from the Nursery: Tracing the Roots of Violence*. The Atlantic Monthly Press.

Katz, Lilian. 1980. *Mothering and Teaching*. In vol. 3 of *Current Topics in Early Childhood Education*. Ablex.

Kendall-Tackett, Kathleen A. 2001. *The Hidden Feelings of Motherhood: Coping with Stress, Depression, and Burnout*. New Harbinger Publications.

King, LaGarrett J. 2020. "Black History Is Not American History: Toward a Framework of Black Historical Consciousness." *Social Education* 84 (6): 335–41.

Klaus, Marshall H., and John H. Kennell. 1976. *Maternal-Infant Bonding: The Impact of Early Separation or Loss on Family Development*. The C. V. Mosby Company.

Kohl, Herbert E. 1984. *Growing Minds: On Becoming a Teacher*. Harper and Row.

Leach, Penelope. 1986. *Your Baby and Child: From Birth to Age Five*. Alfred A. Knopf.

Leboyer, Frederick. 1995. *Birth Without Violence*. Inner Traditions Publishers.

Louv, Richard. 2008. *Last Child in the Woods: Saving Our Children from Nature-Deficit Disorder*. Algonquin Books of Chapel Hill.

Madrid, Antonio, and Dale Pennington. 2000. "Maternal-Infant Bonding and Asthma." *Journal of Prenatal and Perinatal Psychology and Health* 14 (314): 279–90.

Mangione, Peter. 1988. *Respectfully Yours: Magda Gerber's Approach to Professional Infant/Toddler Care*. California Department of Education.

Mercer, Jean. 2006. *Understanding Attachment: Parenting, Child Care, and Emotional Development*. Praeger Publishers.

McKinnon, Colleen. 2024. In-person interview with the author, July 22.

Montessori, Maria. 1912. *The Montessori Method: Scientific Pedagogy as Applied to Child Education in "the Children's Houses" with Additions and Revisions by the Author*. Translated by Anne E. George. Frederick A. Stokes Company.

———. 1949. *The Absorbent Mind*. Theosophical Publishing House.

Muhammad, Gholdy E. 2020. *Cultivating Genius: An Equity Framework for Culturally and Historically Responsive Literacy*. Scholastic.

Muller, Meir, Eliza G. Braden, Susi Long, Gloria Swindler Boutte, and Kamania Wynter-Hoyte. 2022. "Toward Pro-Black Early Childhood Teacher Education." *Young Children* 77 (1). www.naeyc.org/resources/pubs/yc/spring2022/pro-black-ece.

National Association for the Education of Young Children (NAEYC). 2009. *Where We Stand on Professional Preparation Standards*. www.naeyc.org/sites/default/files

References

/globally-shared/downloads/PDFs/resources/position-statements/programStandards.pdf.

———. 2020. *Position Statement: Developmentally Appropriate Practice.* www.naeyc.org/sites/default/files/globally-shared/downloads/PDFs/resources/position-statements/dap-statement_0.pdf.

New Hampshire Pediatric Society Newsletter. n.d. "Media Violence and Medical Literacy."

Nilsson, Lennart. 1980. *A Child Is Born.* Delacorte Press.

Papousek, Mechthild, Michael Schieche, and Harald Wurmser, eds. 2008. *Disorders of Behavioral and Emotional Regulation in the First Years of Life: Early Risks and Intervention in the Developing Parent-Infant Relationship.* Zero to Three.

Petrie, Stephanie, and Sue Owen. 2006. *Authentic Relationships in Group Care for Infants and Toddlers: Resources for Infant Educarers (RIE).* Jessica Kingsley Publishers.

Piaget, Jean. 1973. *The Child and Reality: Problems of Genetic Psychology.* Translated by Arnold Rosin. New York: Grossman Publishers.

———. 1974. *To Understand Is to Invent.* Viking Press.

———. 1976. *The Child and Reality.* Penguin Books.

Ranfos, Lisa, 2024. In person interview with the author, February 17.

Ruopp, Richard, J. Travers, F. Glantz, and C. Coelen. 1979. *Children at the Center: Final Report of the National Day Care Study.* Cambridge, MA: Abt Associates.

Saracho, Olivia N. 2023. "Theories of Child Development and Their Impact on Early Childhood Education and Care." *Early Childhood Education Journal* 51: 15–30. https://doi.org/10.1007/s10643-021-01271-5.

Scattolin, Mônica Ayres de Araújo, Rosa Miranda Resegue, and Maria Conceição do Rosário. 2022. "The Impact of the Environment on Neurodevelopmental Disorders in Early Childhood." *Jornal de Pediatria* 98, supp. 1: S66–S72. https://doi.org/10.1016/j.jped.2021.11.002.

Schaffer, Rudolph. 1978. *Mothering.* Cambridge, MA: Harvard University Press.

Scott, Stephen C. 2017. "Black Excellence: Fostering Intellectual Curiosity in Minority Honors Students at a Predominantly White Research Institution." *Journal of the National Collegiate Honors Council* 18, no. 1 (Spring/Summer): 547.

Sears, William, and Martha Sears. 2001. *The Attachment Parenting Book: A Commonsense Guide to Understanding and Nurturing Your Baby.* Little, Brown.

Sharma, Bhavika, and Bani Narula. 2024. "A Review Study on the Role of Helicopter Parenting in Competitive Societies and Its Effect on Children's Autonomy and Self-Esteem." *International Journal of Interdisciplinary Approaches in Psychology* 2, no. 12 (December): 1–16.

Smith, Janna Malamud. 2003. *A Potent Spell: Mother Love and the Power of Fear.* Houghton Mifflin Company.

References

Sood, Medhavi and Tom Buchanan. 2023. "Helicopter Parenting of Minor Teenagers in India: Scale Development and Consequences." *The Family Journal*, 32 (2): 292–303.

Spock, Benjamin. 1970. *Baby and Child Care*. Pocket Books.

Stern, Daniel. 1977. *The First Relationship: Infant and Mother*. Harvard University Press.

Suomi, Stephen J., Frank C. P. van der Horst, and René van der Veer. 2008. "Rigorous Experiments on Monkey Love: An Account of Harry F. Harlow's Role in the History of Attachment Theory." *Integrative Psychological and Behavioral Science* 42 (4): 354–69.

Thomas, Alexander, Stella Chess, and Herbrt George Birch. 1968. *Temperament and Behavior Disorders in Children*. New York University Press.

Vicedo, Marga. 2017. "Putting Attachment in Its Place: Disciplinary and Cultural Contexts." *European Journal of Developmental Psychology* 14 (6): 684–99. www.tandfonline.com/doi/full/10.1080/17405629.2017.1289838.

Vigdal, Julia Schønning, and Kolbjørn Kallesten Brønnick. 2022. "A Systematic Review of 'Helicopter Parenting' and Its Relationship with Anxiety and Depression." *Frontiers in Psychology* 13:872981.

Viorst, Judith. 1998. *Necessary Losses: The Loves, Illusions, Dependencies, and Impossible Expectations That All of Us Have to Give Up in Order to Grow*. Simon & Schuster.

Vonnegut, Kurt. 1999. *God Bless You, Dr. Kevorkian*. Seven Stories Press.

Vygotsky, Lev. 1978. *Mind in Society: The Development of Higher Psychological Processes*. Harvard University Press.

Warner, Judith. 2005. *Perfect Madness: Motherhood in the Age of Anxiety*. Riverhead.

Warren, Rita. 1977. *Caring: Supporting Children's Growth*. National Association for the Education of Young Children.

Weber, Susan. 2003. "The Lives and Work of Emmi Pikler and Magda Gerber." https://s3.us-east-2.amazonaws.com/waldorf.library.journal.books/Journal_Articles/GW44piklergerber.pdf.

West, Diana. 2007. *The Death of the Grown-Up: How America's Arrested Development Is Bringing Down Western Civilization*. St. Martin's Press.

Winnicott, D. W. 1994. *Talking to Parents*. Addison-Wesley Publishing Company.

Wolpert, Ellen. 2005. *Start Seeing Diversity: The Basic Guide to an Anti-Bias Classroom*. Redleaf Press.

Wynter-Hoyte, Kamania, and Mukkaramah Smith. 2020. "'Hey, Black Child. Do You Know Who You Are?' Using African Diaspora Literacy to Humanize Blackness in Early Childhood Education." *Journal of Literacy Research* 52 (4): 406–31.

Young-Eisendrath, Polly. 2008. *The Self-Esteem Trap: Raising Confident and Compassionate Kids in an Age of Self-Importance*. Little, Brown and Company.

Index

A

abstract thinking, 82
accommodation, 74, 81
accountability system components, 129–130
activities, open-ended, 80–81
Ainsworth, Mary
  biography, 95–96, 97–98, 100, 104–105
  Bowlby and, 96–97, 104
  observations by, 96, 98, 99, 100, 102–104
  resources about, 106
  theories of
    discussion questions about, 105
    mothers in, 98–99, 100–104
    in twenty-first century, 104–105
Allen, Brian, 89
anxious-ambivalent insecure attachment, 103
anxious-avoidant insecure attachment, 103–104
The Anxious Generation (Haidt), 120
attachment
  babies and
    Ainsworth and, 98, 99
    behaviors indicating, 98–99
    Bowlby, 88, 90–91, 92, 100
    discussion questions about, 62–63, 92
    Erikson, 48–49, 50–51
    importance of, 85
    types of attachment, 102–104
  as changing characteristic, 104
  described, 46–47
  infant determinism and, 91
"attachment parenting," 47, 50
autonomy
  development of willpower, 44
  discussion question about, 63
  early childhood as critical in development of, 45
  trust as necessary for, 47

B

babies
  development of trust in grown-ups, xvi–xvii, 46–47, 48
  environments for, 70–71
  learning through feelings by, 48
  learning through senses and physical activity by, 69–70
  materials for, 71
  object permanence and, 69–70
  reactions of, 69
  responding to distress in, 49–50
  separation anxiety, 70, 71–73
  See also under attachment
Bassok, Daphna, 141
beauty, as critical aspect of environment, 31–32
Becoming Attached (Karen), 96–97
behavior(s)
  of babies in Strange Situation
    anxious-ambivalent insecure attachment, 103
    anxious-avoidant insecure attachment, 103–104
    secure attachment, 102–103
  culture and, 100
  indicating attachment, 98–99
  make-believe play and, 118–119
  modeling, 117
  origins of troubled, in late childhood and adolescence, 86
  of parents and unresolved issues from childhoods, 87
Between Parent and Teenager (Ginott), 39
Black American English, 125
Black children
  absorption of messages of White superiority by, 134
  Black joy and, 128, 135
  education and upward mobility of, 125
  mentors for, 131

Index

orality of, 126–127
realities of lives of, xviii
recognition of value of African American culture and contributions and, 125, 128, 132–133, 134, 135
White educational settings as default norm and, 124
See also Hale, Janice E.
"Black Skin, White Theorists: Remembering Hidden Black Early Childhood Scholars" (Broughton), 124
Boutte, Gloria, xviii, 134
Bowlby, John
  Ainsworth and, 96–97, 104
  biography, 85–86
  goal of, 89
  observation and, 86, 87, 88
  psychoanalytic community and, 86, 87, 88
  resources about, 93
  theories of
    attachment, 88, 90–91, 92, 100
    critical questions in, 89
    discontinuity of care, 97
    discussion questions about, 92
    mothers in, 89, 90–91, 97
    overview, 87
    reception of, 87–88
    in twenty-first century, 91–92
Bowman, Barbara, 124–125, 127
Britain, Lory, 16
Broughton, Anthony, xviii, 124

C

Casa dei Bambini (Rome), 28
Chaillé, Christine, 16
change(s), societal adaptation to, xiii
child development
  age continuum for each stage, 68
  culture and, 133
  different expressions of, 127
  learning and, 127
  Saracho on theory of, 5
  theories' partnership with practice, xvii–xviii
  Western perspectives' domination of, 133
Childhood and Society (Erikson), 43, 44

children
  characteristics of most four- and five-year-olds, 56–59
  concentration abilities of, 34
  as constructing knowledge, 67
  early childhood of, as critical in development of trust, autonomy, and initiative, 45
  egocentrism of, 73–74
  interest of, in real work, 33
  literal interpretations of, 76–77
  needs of, xi
  recognition of race by, 134
  scaffolding of other children by, 109–110, 111–113
Chipman, Alice, 9
class size, 127–128
cognitive control, 117–119, 120
cognitive development (Piaget's theories)
  concrete operations and formal operations stages of, 81–82
  overview of, 67–69
  physical development and stages of, 110
  preoperational stage of
    confusion of conservation concepts, 74–75
    egocentrism of children in, 73–74
    focus on one attribute of object or person, 75–77
    importance of open-ended activities and questions, 80–81
    incorrect generalizations, 75
    learning by their direct experiences in life, 74–75
    outdoor time benefits, 78–79
    providing real-world experiences, 80
    unrealistic learning standards and, 79–80
  sensorimotor stage of
    babies' reactions, 69
    environment during, 70–71
    object permanence, 69–70
    separation anxiety, 71–73
cognitive development (Vygotsky's theories)
  importance of play in, 108–109
  importance of social surroundings and interactions in, 110
  language and, 108–109, 113–114

social development and, 108, 114–116
zone of proximal development, 109–110, 117–118
Columbia University, 10
competence of children
    adults "serving children" and, 33, 38–40, 57
    ages four to five, 57
    "attachment parenting" and, 47
    helicopter parents and, 39
    increasing whenever possible, 34
    scaffolding and, 109–110, 111–113
confidence, handling mistakes to build, 59
constructivist model, 14, 16
Coontz, Stephanie, xii
culture
    activities based in, provided by families, 131–132
    as adaptation to environment, 124–125
    behavior and, 100
    Black
        joy in, 128, 135
        orientation toward oral communication, 126–127
        recognition of value of, 125
    child development and, 133
    classroom enrichment with, 131–133
    play and, 133
    transitions in, 25
curiosity, as driver of learning, 25, 67
curricula
    children's curiosity and, 67
    considering individual differences, 60
    constructivist model, 14
    Dewey and, 12, 13, 14, 15–17, 20–25
    emergent model, 14
    focusing, on real tasks, 60–61
    hands-on, described, 16
    observations as basis of, 13, 38
    Piaget and, 79
    providing real-world experiences in, 80
    questions to ask when planning, 20–21
    recognition of value of African American culture and contributions, 125, 128, 132–133, 134, 135
    using documentation to plan, 23–25
    Vygotsky and, 110–113

D

The Death of the Grown-Up: How America's Arrested Development Is Bringing Down Western Civilization (West), 39
developmentally appropriate practice (DAP)
    Dewey as basis for, 14
    fingerpainting example, 138–139
Dewey, John
    as basis for DAP, 14
    biography, 9–11
    resources about, 26
    theories of
        curriculum and, 12, 13, 14, 15–17, 20–25
        discussion questions about, 25–26
        education versus miseducation, 20–24
        helping children make sense of their surroundings and experiences, 17–20
        main ideas in, 11–13
        teacher's role in, 13–15, 24–25
        in twenty-first century, 25
    Vygotsky and, 109
Dewey's Laboratory School: Lessons for Today (Tanner), 11
discussion questions
    attachment theory, 62–63, 92
    autonomy, 63
    Black joy, 135
    Dewey's theories, 25–26
    free play, 83
    involvement of families, 135
    progressive education, 25
    responsibilities of children in classroom, 40
    separation anxiety, 83, 93
    supporting families, 105
    translating "secure base" to child care environment, 105
disequilibrium, 74
documentation, 23–25, 88
dreams, 86

E

early childhood education (ECE)
    benefits of, 4

Index

elements common to most programs of high quality, 139–140
teachers without training in, 140
theories of
    importance of, xv–xvii
    practice and, 3–4
    teaching, 2–3
education
    achievement disparity between Black children and White peers, 126
    as life long, 12
    versus miseducation, 20–24
    progressive, 10, 13–14, 25
    purposes of, 126
    of teachers, 62, 140, 141–142
    upward mobility of Black children and, 125
    White, settings as default norm, 124
educators. *See* teachers
egocentrism, 73–74
Eight Ages of Man. *See under* Erikson, Erik
Elkind, David, 121
emergent curriculum model, 14, 25–26
empathy, attachment and, 47
environments
    for babies, 70–71
    beautiful and interesting, appealing to senses, 31–32
    child-centered, 29–30, 31
    cultural enrichment of, 131–133
    culture as adaptation to, 124–125
    helping children make sense of, 17–20
    interactions with, create learning, 67, 68
    teachers as guardians and custodians of, 31
    translating "secure base" to child care, 105
    in Vygotsky's theories, 110
equilibrium, 74
equipment
    accessibility of, 30, 31
    child-sized, 30
    use of real tools, 30, 60–61
Erikson, Erik
    biography, 43
    Eight Ages of Man
        Autonomy vs. Shame and Doubt, 51–56

        discussion questions about, 62–63
        Initiative vs. Guilt, 56–61
        meeting unmet childhood needs and, 91
        overview of, 44–46
        Trust vs. Mistrust, 45, 46–51
        in twenty-first century, 61–62
        movement through stages, 47
        resources about, 63–64
executive function, 117–119, 120
expectations, setting appropriate, 57–58
Experience and Education (Dewey), 13
experiences
    children learning by their direct, 74–75
    competencies needed by teachers to provide educational, 14
    helping children make sense of, 17–20
    making, educational, 20–24
    planning, using documentation, 23–25
    play as making sense of, 133
    providing real-world, 80
    sensory
        environments that lead to, 31–32
        importance of, 29
        learning by babies and, 69–70

F

families
    cultural activities for students provided by, 131–132
    discussion questions about involvement of, 135
    myths about, xii
    sensitivity of teacher to values and needs of, 12
    supporting, 105
    troubled behaviors in late childhood and adolescence as having origins in, 86
    volunteering in classrooms, 128, 129
feeding babies and attachment, 48–49, 98
fingerpainting lesson, 138–139
flexibility
    of teachers, 36
    of thought by children, 82
Freud, Anna, 43

G

Ginott, Haim, 39
"good old days," xii

H

Haidt, Jonathan, 120
Hale, Janice E.
  biography, 123
  resources about, 136
  theories of
    classroom instruction component, 126–128
    cultural enrichment, 131–133
    discussion questions about, 135
    instructional accountability infrastructure component, 129–130
    in twenty-first century, 133–135
Harlow, Harry, 90–91
helicopter parents, 39, 58
hypothesis, theory and, 5, 6

I

ice cream lessons, 21–24
identity crisis, 44
independence, encouraging, 58, 59
Infancy in Uganda (Ainsworth), 100
infant determinism, 91
initiative, early childhood as critical in development of, 45
in loco parentis committees, 129–130
intellectual growth and physical development, 68
interaction, best learning with, 12

J

Jones, Elizabeth, 66–67

K

Kagan, Jerome, xi, 91–92
Karen, Robert, 96–97
King, LaGarrett J., 128
Kohl, Herbert, 140

L

language
  Black American English, 125
  cognitive development and, 108–109, 113–114
  screen time and, 120
Last Child in the Woods (Louv), xiii
learning
  accommodation and, 74, 81
  child development and, 127
  curiosity as driver of, 25, 67
  by direct experiences in life, 74–75
  by doing, 33, 67
  executive function and, 117
  interactions with environment create, 67, 68
  pressures of standards of, 79–80
  by repetition, 33
  sensory experiences as best way of, 29
  social and cultural contexts effect on, 133
  through feelings of babies, 48
  through play, 68
  through senses and physical activity, 69–70
Louv, Richard, xiii

M

make-believe play, 118–119
materials
  accessibility of, 30, 31
  for babies, 71
  tools, 30, 60–61
maternal deprivation, 90–91, 97
McKinnon, Colleen, 132–133
Mead, Margaret, xiv
media, influence of, xii
mentors
  male, for Black children, 131
  for teachers, 130
Mercer, Jean, 91
miseducation versus education, 20–24
mistakes
  children ages four to five and, 57
  handling, to build confidence, 59
Montessori, Maria

Index

biography, 27–28
influence of, 29, 67, 77
resources about, 40–41
theories of
  beautiful and interesting environments that appeal to senses, 31–32
  child-centered environments, 29–30, 31
  competence and responsibility of children, 33–34, 37, 38
  discussion questions about, 40
  main ideas in, 28–29
  observation in, 35, 36–38
  scheduling large blocks of open-ended time, 34–36
  use of real tools, 30
mothers
  theories of Ainsworth, 98–99, 100–104
  theories of Bowlby, 89, 90–91, 97
My Pedagogic Creed (Dewey), 12–13, 25

N

National Association for the Education of Young Children (NAEYC), 128, 133, 137
National Council of Teachers of English, 135
natural world, benefits of time in, 78–79
"nature-deficit disorder," xiii
The New York Times, 105
nurturing care, interrelated and indivisible components of, 46

O

object permanence, 69–70
observation(s)
  Ainsworth and, 96, 98, 99, 100, 102–104
  as basis of curriculum, 13, 38
  Bowlby and, 86, 87, 88
  importance of, 13
  as jumping-off point to knowing children's needs and wants, 37–38
  Montessori on, 35, 36–38
  Piaget and, 66, 67, 79
  reflecting on, 36–37
  scaffolding and, 109–110
  Vygotsky and, 108, 109–110, 113
open-ended time, 34–36
orality, 126–127
outdoors, xiii, 78–79

P

parents
  of anxious-ambivalent insecure attached babies, 103
  assistance to, 89
  "attachment," 47, 50
  constantly giving in to children's demands, 61–62
  feelings of competence as, 62
  helicopter, 39, 58
  pressuring children to succeed, 58
  of securely attached babies, 102–103
  separation anxiety and, 71–73
  as targets to blame, xiii–xiv
  understanding of child's developmental stages by, 72–73
  unresolved issues from own childhoods of, 87
  Victorian upper-middle-class English, 85
Parker, Kim, xviii
Perfect Madness: Motherhood in the Age of Anxiety (Warner), 58
Perry Preschool Project, 88
physical development and intellectual growth, 68, 110
Piaget, Jean
  basis of curricula, 79
  biography, 65–66
  influence of, 108
  Montessori and, 29, 67, 77
  observations by, 66, 67, 79
  resources about, 84
  theories of
    concrete operations and formal operations stages of cognitive development, 81–82
    discussion questions about, 83
    overview, 67–69
    in twenty-first century, 82–83
    See also cognitive development (Piaget's theories)
Pipher, Mary, xi

play
  cognitive development and, 108–109
  culture and, 133
  discussion question about importance of, 83
  large blocks of time for free, 77–78
  learning through, 68
  make-believe, 118–119
  as making sense of experiences, 133
practice and theory, 137–139
progressive education
  criticisms of, children given freedom without guidance, 13–14
  discussion questions about, 25
  as reaction to nineteenth-century education, 10
  See also Dewey, John; Montessori, Maria; Piaget, Jean; Vygotsky, Lev
psychoanalysis, 87, 88
psychoanalytic community, 86, 96
psychosocial development stages, overview of, 44–46
purpose, sense of, development of, 44, 59

Q

questions, open-ended, 80–81

R

race
  classroom conversations about, 135
  discussion questions about, involving families, 135
  recognition of, by children, 134
Ranfos, Lisa, 71, 130
Redbook, xiv
reflections
  on Dewey's theory about teacher's role, 15
  on observations, 36–37
Reggio Emilia schools, 32, 108
repetition, learning by, 33
research studies, quantitative vs. qualitative, 88
responsibilities of children, 33–34, 40
reversibility, 82
rhesus monkeys' studies, 90–91

S

Salter, Mary Dinsmore. *See* Ainsworth, Mary
Saracho, Olivia, xvii, 5
scaffolding
  by children, 109–110
  executive function and, 117–118
  by teachers, 115–116
Scattolin, Mônica, 45–46
The Science and Clinical Practice of Attachment Theory (Allen), 89
screen time, 120
secure attachment, 102–103
"secure base" theory, 102–103, 105
self-regulation skills, 117–119, 120
sensory experiences
  environments that lead to, 31–32
  importance of, 29
  learning by babies and, 69–70
separation anxiety
  discussion questions about, 83, 93
  helping parents understand, 72–73
  object permanence and, 70
  responding to, 71–72
small-group work, 78
snacktime, 78
social development
  cognitive development and, 108, 114–116
  discussion questions about, 120–121
  make-believe play and, 118–119
social media platforms, 120
society
  examples of adaptation to changes in, xiii
  teachers as shapers of, 12–13, 25
  teaching children to live in, 25
  violence in, xii
Spitz, René, 90
Spock, Benjamin, 61
starting-point for education, child's instincts and powers as, 12
story time, 78
Strange Situation, 101–104
success, parents pressuring children for, 58

Index

T

Tanner, Laurel, 11
teachers
　allocation of large blocks of time for free play by, 77–78
　confidence of, 15, 16–17
　education of, 62, 140, 141–142
　flexibility of, 36
　as guardians and custodians of environment, 31
　helping parents understand child's developmental stages, 72–73
　importance of enabling children to do things for themselves, 33–34, 38–40, 57
　instructional leaders to work with, 129
　in loco parentis committees and, 129–130
　mentorships and, 130
　modeling behavior by, 117
　as nurturers of inquiry, not providers of information, 67–68
　as observers, 13, 35
　ratio to students, 127–128
　scaffolding by, 109–110
　sensitivity of, to values and needs of families, 12
　as shapers of society, 12–13, 25
　small-group work and, 78
　tendency of, to plan all activities, 34
　theory and practice, 137–139
　using own knowledge to expand children's knowledge, 17–20
theory/theories
　defining, 4–5
　developing from research and observation, 6–7
　hypothesis and, 5, 6
　practice and, 137–139
　Saracho on child development, 5
tools, use of real, 60–61
trust
　attachment and, 47
　development of, xvi–xvii, 46–48
　early childhood as critical in development of, 45
　as necessary for autonomy, 47
　parts of, 46

U

University of Chicago, 9–10

V

Vicedo, Marga, 89
violence, in society, xii
Visions for Children, 123
Vonnegut, Kurt, 105
Vygotsky, Lev
　biography, 107
　curriculum planning and, 110–113
　Dewey and, 109
　influence of, 107–108
　Montessori and, 29
　observation and, 108, 109–110, 113
　resources about, 121
　theories of
　　cornerstone of, 107
　　discussion questions about, 120–121
　　executive function, 117–119
　　learning as interactive experience, 108–109, 113–116
　　in twenty-first century, 119–120
　　zone of proximal development, 109–113, 117–120
　See also cognitive development (Vygotsky's theories)

W

Warner, Judith, 58
The Way We Never Were (Coontz), xii
West, Diana, 39
willpower, development of, 44

Y

Young-Eisendrath, Polly, 61–62

Z

zone of proximal development (ZPD), 109–113, 117–120